SPRING S

L.A.

INSIDE OUT

L.A.

The
Architecture
and
Interiors
of
America's
Most
Colorful
City

INSIDE OUT

Paddy Calistro and Betty Goodwin

Photographs by Grey Crawford

Afterword by Michael Rotondi

Designed by Alexander Isley Design

VIKING STUDIO BOOKS

VIKING STUDIO BOOKS
Published by the Penguin Group
Viking Penguin, a division of Penguin Books USA Inc.,
375 Hudson Street, New York, New York 10014, U.S.A.
Penguin Books Ltd, 27 Wrights Lane,
London W8 5TZ, England
Penguin Books Australia Ltd, Ringwood,
Victoria, Australia
Penguin Books Canada Ltd, 10 Alcorn Avenue, Suite 300,
Toronto, Ontario, Canada M4V 3B2
Penguin Books (N.Z.) Ltd, 182–190 Wairau Road,
Auckland 10, New Zealand

Penguin Books Ltd, Registered Offices:
Harmondsworth, Middlesex, England

First published in 1992 by Viking Penguin,
a division of Penguin Books USA Inc.

1 3 5 7 9 10 8 6 4 2

LIBRARY OF CONGRESS CATALOGING IN PUBLICATION DATA
Calistro, Paddy, and Betty Goodwin
L.A. inside out : the architecture and interiors of America's most
colorful city / Paddy Calistro and Betty Goodwin ; photographs by
Grey Crawford : designed by Alexander Isley.
p.   cm.
ISBN 0-670-83950-7
1. Los Angeles (Calif.)—Pictorial works.   2. Architecture—
California—Los Angeles—Pictorial works. 3. Interior decoration—
California—Los Angeles—Pictorial works. I. Goodwin, Betty.
II. Title.
F869.L843C353   1992
720′.9794′94—dc20   91–45373

Printed in Japan

Endpaper artwork courtesy Seaver Center for Western History Research,
Los Angeles County Museum of Natural History

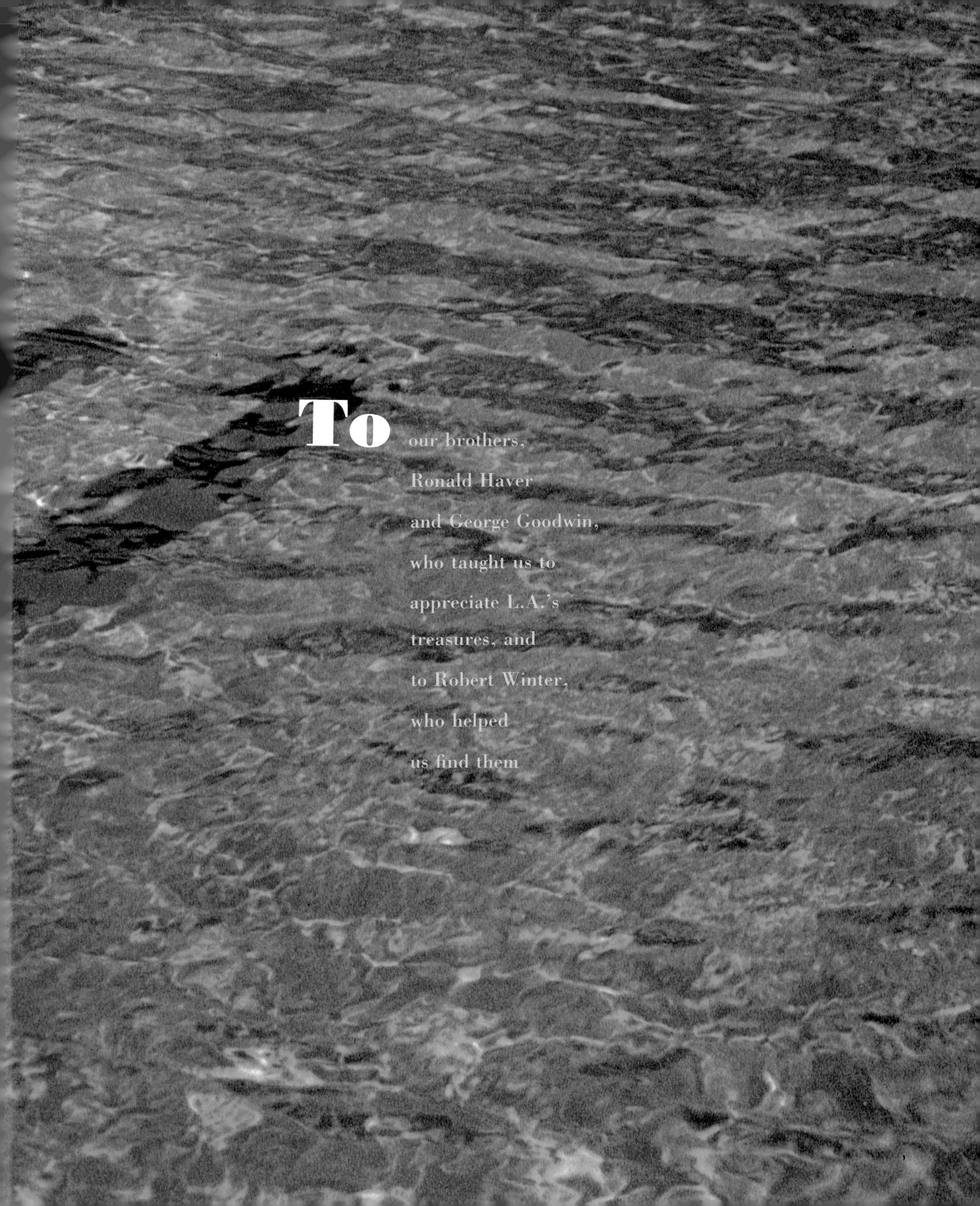

To our brothers,
Ronald Haver
and George Goodwin,
who taught us to
appreciate L.A.'s
treasures, and
to Robert Winter,
who helped
us find them

ACKNOWLEDGMENTS

We are thankful that our publisher, Michael Fragnito, recognized the vitality of Los Angeles and its impact on American culture. He also knew that it takes a journalist to get a story and two journalists to tackle the book he envisioned.

As reporters, we consolidated our most valued possessions—our Rolodexes—and began interviewing hundreds of people who enlightened us and led us to the only-in-L.A. homes we found. We met with historians, realtors, architects, artists, designers, preservationists, socialites, antique dealers—even a rabbi, a priest, and an astrologer.

Through Occidental College's architectural historian, Robert Winter, who helped in countless ways, we met another "angel," Richard Mouck, a true L.A.-lover, who opened some special doors for us. UCLA architectural historian Thomas Hines shared his knowledge freely.

Dion Neutra, Eric Wright, and Wallace L. Neff, descendants of three of the city's great architects, all generously gave of their time. So did Richard Koshalek, director of the Museum of Contemporary Art; Rob Singer, of the Los Angeles County Museum of Art; Los Angeles Conservancy president Margaret Bach; William Mason, of the Museum of Natural History of Los Angeles County; Tom Owen, the Los Angeles Public Library's specialist on California; Randall Makinson, of Gamble House; Jeffrey Springer, of the Automobile Club of Southern California; the Seaver Center at the Museum of Natural History; Amy Meyer and Jenny Watts, of the Huntington Library, Art Collections and Botanical Gardens; Craig Klyver, of the Southwest Museum; William Lahay, of the Pasadena Public Library; The Walt Disney Co., Dace Taub, of the Department of Special Collections, University of Southern California Library; and David Rapoza, John Heller, David Cameron, Andy Cohen, Gloria List, Peter Kamnitzer, Janie Beggs, Strother MacMinn, Norman M. Klein, Julia Winston, Jack Hoffman, Minto Keaton, Neil Sandberg, Steve Breuer, Rabbi Harvey Fields, Melvyn Kinder, Marian Hall, Neil Feineman, Rosario Perry, Ron Rindge, Monsignor Francis J. Weber, Jim Zaferis, Mika and Andreas Kyprianides, Shirley Wilson, Ann Salisbury, Linda Shulman, Harris Shepard, David Moss, Sabato Fiorello, Joanne Fradkin, Astrid Ellersieck, Murray Burns, Planaria Price, Miller Fong, Ted Tanaka and Diana Ho, Norman Neuerberg, Jon and Janis Jerde, Lori Erenberg, Tim and Janet Walker, Charlotte Laubach, Pamela Seager, Donnis Galvan, Deborah Geltman, Steven Ehrlich, Amber Haack, Ed Leffingwell, Peter and Eileen Norton, Virginia Kazor, Jacqueline Green, Carol Meyer, Cleo Baldon, Rip Cronck, Christopher Cox, Howard Green, Ray Kappe, Aida Thibiant, Ann Videriksen, Howard Alexander, Judy Henning, Howard Frank, Harriet Gold, Larry Payne, Paul Rosenfield, Jacqueline Cohen, Joan Luther, and Patricia Fox.

When we got in our cars and covered what seemed like every block in Los Angeles County and came across houses that were irresistible, many homeowners bravely opened their doors and welcomed us—an amazing testament to the friendliness of Angelenos. We thank all the homeowners named in the pages of our book who allowed us to enter their worlds and photograph. We are especially grateful to Van-Martin Rowe, Laurie Lee Warner, Bruce Meyer, Stephen Harby, and Peter Bartlett for their extra efforts.

Laura Hull was a wonderful and hardworking addition to our photographic team.

Special thanks to the illustrious newspaper and magazine editors who not only contributed leads, tips, and encouragement but also were always understanding when we were up against deadlines, especially Mary Rourke and Janice Mall of the *Los Angeles Times* and Jean Penn at *Los Angeles* magazine. Also our gratitude to Paul Dean and John Dart of the *Los Angeles Times* and to Judy Bloom and Jeff Silverman for their enthusiasm and support.

This book took so long to come to fruition, yet our family and friends never gave up on us. You are the true treasures in our lives.

Graphic designer Alexander Isley and his associate, Barbara Sullivan, turned hundreds of pictures and thousands of words into a book more beautiful than we could ever have imagined.

L.A. Inside Out would never have become a reality without the work of two special women and one special man: our insightful editor, Barbara Williams, whose joyful spirit is contagious; our determined agent, Gayle Benderoff, whose instincts can always be trusted; and our indefatigable photographer, Grey Crawford, who made every day of photography a pleasure.

Finally, for their contributions far beyond the call of duty (and always without a bill), our love and gratitude to Eugene Goodwin and Scott McAuley.

B.G.G.
P.C.M.

Los Angeles County, 1992

CONTENTS

L.A. Today

The name Los Angeles conjures up many images. It's a metropolis, fully shaped in the twentieth century, where creativity, futurism, escapism, glamour, and the unconventional collide. It's the spirit of a new and constantly changing American frontier expressed naturally in the way people live and in the style of their homes. It's a test lab for all that is modern, a place where innovative minds continually redefine the avant-garde. What is most indigenous is new, constantly evolving design.

No single picture does justice to Los Angeles. You have to get in a car—L.A.'s long-established symbol of freedom—to comprehend its vast size and myriad aesthetic riches, both God-given and man-made. At every turn, the city presents visual inspirations. Charming Craftsman-style bungalows, rambling ranch houses, and steel-and-glass aeries vie for attention along twisting canyon roads, beachside highways, and gridlike city blocks. Architectural references to the city's early Spanish and Mexican past blanket the area like the sun on a hot summer day and give L.A. its most familiar style—the terra-cotta rooftops and the pink or white stucco walls that appear on houses, hotels, even gas stations.

Your senses can be assaulted by storefronts and watering holes that are as flamboyant as the Academy Awards, by freeway murals meant to be read at 55 miles per hour, and by the in-your-face graffiti left by gang members. Those with closed minds may deride the city's foibles, overstatements, and gaucheries and not look any further. But appreciation for things fun and imaginative is high art in Los

LEFT: L.A. interiors bring together diverse cultural, historical, and environmental elements. In his Venice Beach house (see page 281), architect Greg Lombardi merges art deco and modernist designs in this striking entryway.

Angeles, regarded as seriously as more traditional cultural pursuits. All kinds of buildings speak to a sense of play—you can live in a Japo-Swiss bungalow, work in an office building shaped like an ocean liner, dance the night away in a Mayan temple, pray in a mini Taj Mahal, and dine in view of a colossal hot dog.

The semi-arid climate is the nucleus of L.A.'s charisma, sustaining the abundant vegetation, liberated lifestyle, and healthy population. A life as lush as the landscape has always been the city's lure. At home, the ultimate L.A. indulgence is to open wide the doors and windows and let the outdoors in. Throughout the years, architects have sought ways to make the inside interchangeable with the outside. During the first years of the city's settlement, its adobe structures adjoined a central

plaza. Craftsman architects communed with nature by constructing open-air sleeping porches. The tradition of the Spanish courtyard continually resurfaces in mansions, bungalows, and apartment buildings. Modernists made walls disappear with great expanses of glass. And in the endless search for ways to blur the lines between indoors and out, people have always prized all forms of water elements—pools, ponds, fountains—in their homes and their gardens.

The plants and trees that grow so abundantly on the landscape may be the inspiration for it all, but like many Angelenos, they come from somewhere else. Roses, citrus trees, bougainvillea, eucalyptuses—they're all immigrants, even the ubiquitous palm tree. Only one species of palm—the California fan palm, or Washingtonia—is indigenous. A thousand more species were imported from tropical and subtropical regions.

The intense colors of the scenery add to the visual impact, and purple sunsets, acid-green lawns, and electric-orange birds of paradise are commonplace. On perfect

ABOVE: Frequently, homeowners go to great lengths to make their buildings noticeable. Here, the message is anything but subtle. On the sands of Santa Monica Beach, Rosario Perry's fluorescent-colored home has become something of a landmark. RIGHT: The downtown skyline, as seen from a hilltop in East Los Angeles. Residential neighborhoods spread in all directions from the office towers clustered near the area where the original pueblo was founded. BELOW: L.A.'s City Hall tower is one of the most familiar sights in the downtown civic center, visible from all surrounding freeways. But here, a tongue-in-cheek design for a hamburger stand on Melrose Avenue spoofs the building. The eatery called Burger That Ate L.A. was designed by Solberg and Lowe in 1989 and fea-

tures a miniature City Hall poised next to a giant hamburger with a missing bite. FAR RIGHT: Much of the city's character comes from the colorful people who live, work, and play here. Their creativity emerges at every turn and in the most unexpected places. This mural-in-progress was spotted on a wall in a Venice Beach alley. The bare torso seen here was eventually transformed into a much-larger-than-life portrait of legendary rock star Jim Morrison.

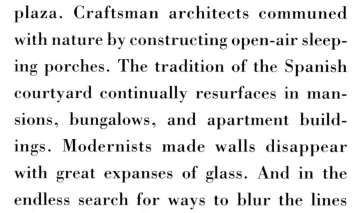

days, and there are many, the ocean breezes cleanse the air, and the sun sparkles on sidewalks emblazoned with stars and star names—Hollywood's ode to its own luminaries—and on ever-present backyard swimming pools, chrome fenders, and the everyday parade of dark eyeglasses. Somehow, on these ideal days, smog seems like a distant bad dream. That's when you can admire the storybook houses, each with its requisite orange tree, and when the whole city looks like a high-budget movie set.

At the heart of the sprawl are the Angelenos, culturally diverse and proudly multiethnic. That is a claim many other American cities can make, but Los Angeles is the world's only major metropolis with no single ethnic majority. L.A.'s proximity to Mexico and the Pacific Rim countries means that there is a tremendous influx of newcomers from these areas. They and other ethnic groups have an important voice in shaping the city's culture. Since everyone and everything here has roots somewhere else, that explains the varied styles of art, fashion, music, food, and, naturally, architecture. Unenlightened critics mock L.A.'s frustrating lack of a singular style of anything, but it's precisely the mix that creates the city's identity.

The geographical and cultural hub of Southern California, Los Angeles County has a population of 8.8 million, which is expected to more than double in twenty years. It is officially the nation's largest metropolis. Big, powerful, self-energized—and growing every which way with no end in sight—L.A. is an international financial and cultural capital (though not California's capital). Strategically poised at the crossroads of Eastern and Western societies, L.A. is the prototype of the twenty-first-century city.

One can best understand L.A. by getting to its heart. So this book opens the doors to houses that show how history and contemporary culture forge the city's uncommon style.

LEFT: A few paces from where prehistoric animals once disappeared into La Brea Tar Pits and, centuries later, where the city's first settlers collected the tar to protect their roofs rises the Los Angeles County Museum of Art. The newest wing, built in 1986 by Hardy Holzman and Pfeiffer, fronts on palmy Wilshire Boulevard. ABOVE: Angelenos express themselves in big ways. In 1987, L.A.'s celebrated freeway muralist Kent Twitchell painted this image of fellow L.A. painter Don Bachardy on an exterior wall in the backyard of the home of art patrons Peter and Eileen Norton. ABOVE RIGHT: More ordinary but no less colorful artwork appears on brightly painted fruit and vegetable barrels in downtown's historic Olvera Street. BELOW: For the millions of tourists who can't resist taking home a bit of Los Angeles, kitschy items such as this surfer-in-a-shake-up-snowball are prized. Many Angelenos with pride of place and a sense of humor make sport of collecting them too.

1

In the summer of 1781,
a tiny village in the fertile
Porciuncula River valley
was named El Pueblo de
Nuestra Señora la Reina
de Los Angeles de
Porciuncula by the Spanish

Beginnings

governor of Alta California,
the vast region north
of Mexico's Baja California.
Framed by foothills and arid
flatlands and cooled by
ocean breezes, this primitive
enclave was one of the last
outposts of imperial Spain.
Spanish rule would come

LEFT: Mission San Gabriel Arcángel, the fourth in a chain of coastal mission settlements, was founded in 1771 but moved to its present site in 1775. The *campanario*, with its six unique bells, quickly became a symbol of the mission and was often illustrated on postcards like this one. ABOVE RIGHT: Here, a Los Angeles artist interprets a wedding party arriving on horseback at a Southern California *rancho*, circa 1843. An adobe house can be seen in the distance. TOP RIGHT: The orange is intrinsic to the heritage of Los Angeles. Indeed, Father Tomás Sánchez is credited with planting the first orange trees at the mission in 1804, but it wasn't until midcentury that the largest orange grove in the United States—some 2500 trees—was cultivated here by William Wolfskill.

to an end here in 1822, but the Town of Our Lady, the Queen of the Angels of Porciuncula would survive and expand to unimaginable proportions. El Pueblo has all but disappeared, yet its remnants—including the Plaza Church on Main Street (1822) and the Avila Adobe on Olvera Street (1818)—are the geographic heart of the 4000 square miles now called Los Angeles County. Today this vestige of colonial Spain lies in the shadows of Los Angeles City Hall and downtown's steel-and-glass skyline.

The Los Angeles pueblo was established 9 miles west of Mission San Gabriel

BELOW: Fiestas were a vibrant part of *rancho* life, but only for the wealthy few. Here, watercolorist Alexander F. Harmer depicts a festive scene, circa 1840.

Arcángel (founded in 1771), the first Spanish settlement in today's Los Angeles County. San Gabriel was the fourth of twenty-one Franciscan missions built along California's coastal trail, El Camino Real, at a site selected by Padre Junípero Serra, long regarded as the founder of the mission chain. The Spaniards envisioned missions as part of an elaborate expansionist scheme that would convert Native Americans into Catholics, colonists, and a convenient work force. Coexisting with military presidios to occupy the new territory and protect Mexico from feared invasions by Russia, France, and Britain, the missions became *the* significant cultural, reli-

ABOVE RIGHT: A trio of palm trees towers above the arches of Mission San Fernando, the second mission established in the Los Angeles area. In its earliest days, the mission's land was dotted with magnificent Washingtonia palms, California's only indigenous species.
ABOVE, FAR RIGHT: The Italianate-style Pico House (1870), once a busy hotel, still stands on Main Street in the Plaza near today's civic center. It was named for Don Pío Pico, the last Mexican governor of California.

gious, and agricultural institution for the earliest Californians.

The padres acted as self-styled architects for the mission complexes. Each mission included storehouses, a kitchen, a refectory, living quarters, and workshops, with a chapel as the centerpiece. Lacking the materials and skilled artisans to erect anything grandiose, the padres stuck to designs that were typically plain and pragmatic.

The primary building material of the missions was brick, made from adobe. These handmade blocks of sun-dried mud and straw were first used in the ancient Middle East, as early as 7000 B.C., and later transported by the Moors to southern Spain. Crude yet functional, adobe kept

buildings cool in hot weather and warm when temperatures fell. The whitewashed mission walls were often six feet thick. Arches were low and rounded to support the weight of the bricks. Wide, overhanging eaves kept the structures cool and protected the adobe from damaging rains, while rooftops were sheathed with the undulating red clay tiles so typical of Spanish architecture.

Because adobe was too heavy to support towering campaniles, the legendary mission bells were suspended in *campanarios*—short, flat walls crowned with a parapet and cut with arched niches. Unlike other mission structures, most of the mission churches were constructed of stone or fired brick, the preferred building materials of the Spanish. *Corredores*, outdoor hallways similar to cloisters, defined by

evenly spaced arches, connected the buildings, which were usually designed around central patios containing a fountain, rose gardens, grapevines, and live oak, alder, and cottonwood trees. In lieu of craftsmen to carve stone in the ornate Spanish Churrigueresque tradition, the friars painted the chapels' decorative trompe l'oeil details—the columns, niches, moldings, and flourishes—in vivid shades of orange, chartreuse, rose, turquoise, gold, and terra-cotta.

Indeed, the distinctive beauty of the California missions resulted from this synergy of Hispanic Old World classicism and the rigors of a primitive New World. While the mission padres were occupied with spiritual conversions and the development of a self-sustaining economic enterprise, they never sacrificed grace for function. The result was a purity of design that has become an architectural trademark of California. Despite a history that links the missions to the exploitation and eventual loss of California's Native American culture, their aesthetic influence endures.

Within twenty years, Mission San Gabriel was a thriving agricultural center and home to thousands of converted Gabrielino Indians, as the indigenous tribes came to be known. In 1797, San Fernando

ABOVE LEFT: A wooden dovecote housing a flock of doves still stands on the back acres of Adobe Leonis (see page 31), which prospered in the late nineteenth century. The birds are just part of the menagerie that thrives on the property today. ABOVE: Huge oak trees form a backdrop for the beautiful Monterey-style Adobe Leonis. Espíritu Leonis, the Indian woman who married Miguel Leonis and lived with him at the adobe, died in 1906, one of the last of the region's Fernandeno Indians. RIGHT: Mission San Gabriel Arcángel looked very different from the other missions, being somewhat fortresslike, with capped buttresses. It has been compared in appearance to the cathedral of Córdoba, Spain, homeland of Father Antonio Cruzado, the padre who supervised the building of the mission's original church. The mission was surrounded by fertile soil, so the settlement became an important agricultural center.

Rey de España, the seventeenth mission in the string, was founded 20 miles to the northwest, the equivalent of about a day's journey by horse. More refined in its architecture than the bulkier San Gabriel, San Fernando became the second mission within Los Angeles County.

During those same years, El Pueblo developed its own culture, which was neither religious nor military but rather an important civilian settlement supporting the missions. To attract settlers to the Los Angeles pueblo, the Spanish Crown turned to young male farmers, skilled laborers, and craftsmen from Mexico's impoverished regions of Sonora and Sinaloa. They were offered the chance to start a new life in Alta California, with the guarantee of regular rations, cattle, tools, clothing, a moratorium on taxes, a salary, and the added promise of eventually owning the land they worked.

Only eleven men and their families were willing to take the risk. In the fall of 1781, a month and a half before George Washington defeated the British at Yorktown, forty-four men, women, and children—descendants of Indians, Africans, and Spaniards—made the difficult journey north, becoming in effect Los Angeles's founding families. And along with them they brought their Mexican way of life—food, clothing, music, dances, art forms, and language—which has steadfastly sur-

vived as an integral part of Los Angeles's modern culture.

El Pueblo, by decree of the Spanish governor, was about 27 miles square, and each home sat on a small plot facing a large central plaza. The original houses were huts constructed of bundles of willow tied with tule. In a few years' time, they were replaced with adobe brick structures with thatch roofs waterproofed with *brea*, or tar, from nearby prehistoric pools, now a monument known, albeit redundantly, as La Brea Tar Pits. Each home had a small altar in its front yard festooned with family treasures, where padres would stop to bestow blessings. Religious services were held in the open plaza until the first church was completed.

A new era emerged when the first Spanish land grants for vast expanses of pasture were given to three soldiers, the largest parcel being more than 150,000 acres, extending from what is now Long Beach to Anaheim. In all, the Spanish issued about twenty grants, absolutely free, with the understanding that the land would be used to raise cattle and that eventually title would be given to the rancher.

Together, these huge *ranchos* supported 12,500 head of cattle, and they were fast making Los Angeles the most important commercial center in California. The Mexican Revolution, in 1822, brought with it

the secularization of the missions (1833), and the new Mexican government granted nearly five hundred additional land grants in order to develop a healthy agricultural stronghold. Los Angeles was witnessing the first manifestation of its urban sprawl: *ranchos* large and small spread throughout the vast lands surrounding the tiny pueblo.

At the same time, the Indians who had not fled the area or perished from the white man's diseases were left to become underpaid laborers at the mercy of wealthy *rancheros*. These land bosses became the aristocracy, and a few lived a resplendent life in their adobe *casas* filled with European furniture and china imported via ships that sailed around Cape Horn. From 1830 to 1860, *rancho* society thrived and early California legends romanticized the lives of the prosperous *dons* and *doñas*. They relished in frequent celebration, and their rodeos, fandangos, and fiestas became part of the idealized Spanish colonial heritage so intrinsic to the lore of the West. Yet, like the Southern plantations, the *ran-*

chos were doomed to extinction.

Depressed cattle prices coupled with alternating droughts and floods brought the *rancho* era to a close. By the time the Mexican national period ended and California was ceded to the United States (1848) and achieved statehood (1850), the Californios of Los Angeles would start to become slowly Americanized—as would their adobes.

In Monterey, the former capital of California, an architectural evolution was tak-

ing place. The first adobe houses with redwood frames were built, strong enough to support a second story and a columned double veranda that protected the mud bricks from water erosion. In effect, these buildings represented the first blending of East and West Coast colonial architecture. While "Monterey-style" houses were rare in Los Angeles, wood refinements were introduced to Los Angeles's adobe homes in the form of shingle roofs. The first wood came from the burgeoning Northern California lumber industry. By the early 1850s, adobe was considered a vestige of the past, and was being replaced with all-wooden and all-brick buildings. A sawmill opened in nearby San Bernardino, and red brick was being fired locally.

The style of the city changed again with the arrival of two railway lines—the Southern Pacific (1876) and Santa Fe (1886)—both competing for customers with bargain rates. At one point, you could travel to Los Angeles from Kansas City for a dollar. Easterners and, in even larger numbers, Midwesterners flocked to the region by the tens of thousands. The population boom of the 1880s brought retirees, health seekers, wealthy vacationers, and dreamers, all enamored more with the sunny skies than with any notion of Mexican culture. An active Los Angeles Chamber of Commerce, founded in 1873, extolled the city's invig-

ABOVE: Today, El Pueblo de Los Angeles is a state historic park, containing some of Los Angeles's oldest buildings, including, at the far right of this historic photo, Plaza Church on Main Street. Originally named La Iglesia de Nuestra Señora la Reina de Los Angeles (The Church of Our Lady the Queen of the Angels), the Mission-style structure was completed in 1822 but has been rebuilt and restored over the years. The Franciscan padres from Mission San Gabriel donated cattle and barrels of brandy to raise money for the original construction. ABOVE CENTER: In the gardens of Rancho Los Alamitos, which is one of the area's oldest existing adobe dwellings (see page 25), flowering plants and lush greenery still provide a sense of the vibrant colors that pervaded early Los Angeles. ABOVE, FAR RIGHT: Other early adobes are still private residences today. These potted succulents are reminders of the tremendous native cactus garden that once surrounded this early-nineteenth-century home.

orating climate. Boxcars of the region's finest crop—oranges—were being shipped to state fairs throughout the nation as well as the World's Columbian Exposition of 1893 in Chicago. And Pasadena's Tournament of Roses conveyed the message that flowers could bloom here all year round. In addition, tourists willingly joined the propaganda campaign: the hand-tinted postcards (often published by the enterprising railroad companies) they sent back home to friends and family celebrated Los Angeles's sunshine, flowers, and bucolic scenery.

Along with their suitcases, these newcomers brought the desire to build homes that looked just like the ones they left behind. Ornate Italianate, Queen Anne, and Eastlake dwellings sprouted in newly minted suburbs that radiated from the new downtown. In homes of the well-heeled, gingerbread trim was often excessive—pseudo-Chinese balustrades, Moorish cupolas, fish-scale shingles. These flourishes were frequently amplified in outlandish shades of pinks, reds, and greens. The grandest houses climbed three stories, complete with formal drawing rooms. But Victorian formality was clearly incompatible with the untamed spirit of Los Angeles and its great outdoors. By the end of the century, Victorian architecture would be replaced with a style more suited to the climate, terrain, and lifestyle.

RANCHO LOS ALAMITOS

The relentless sounds of industrial Long Beach, with its freeways, airport, and seaport, seem to fade away at the gates of Rancho Los Alamitos. Peaceful gardens and groves of pepper trees surround the adobe house that *ranchero* Juan José Nieto built around 1800. The home is probably the oldest residence in Southern California. It is ensconced on a tiny portion of the 167,000-acre Spanish land grant, Los Coyotes, that was awarded in 1790 to Juan's father, Manuel Nieto, a corporal in the Spanish army. By far the largest grant given by the Spanish government, it extended from what today is Long Beach Harbor all the way east to the Anaheim home of Mickey Mouse.

In 1842, Abel Stearns purchased a 28,000-acre portion of the land grant for $6,000, the first of many acquisitions that would result in a major ranching empire. He protected the adobe core of the home by covering it with a gabled and shingled roof and adding a wood-frame wing. The great drought of 1865 brought an end to Stearns's prosperity, however, killing more than 40,000 head of cattle, and he lost his homestead. In 1878, the home was leased to the Bixbys, a family whose descendants would eventually own it and live in it until it was finally deeded, in 1968, to the City of Long Beach to be maintained as a historic landmark.

Today, Rancho Los Alamitos is decorated with many original heirlooms that have been passed down through generations of Bixbys. In a long hall near the main en-

LEFT: The Bixby family, the last inhabitants of Rancho Los Alamitos, spent many hours in the billiard room, where the mood was casual and the furniture strictly informal. A

large billiard table dominated the room, and numerous family portraits were proudly displayed. Here, a red wicker chair is positioned before a window that overlooks the front porch. ABOVE: On the sloping front lawn, a 100-year-old Moreton Bay fig tree extends its branches toward the house. Building upon the porches of earlier occupants, Fred and Florence Bixby created the current expansive front porch around 1908.

trance, separating bedrooms from public rooms, longhorn steer horns and a pair of hand-carved Chinese chairs welcome visitors and also set the mood for the eclectic decor that lies within. Indian blankets and rugs, overstuffed 1940s sofas covered in textured upholstery, pottery from the 1930s, and delicate Victorian pieces are blended in perfect harmony, each a suggestion of a Bixby from generations past. The rooms where the Bixbys spent their casual hours are the most vibrant. A Western theme pervades, with Western art and artifacts such as blankets, beadwork, and cowboy bronzes all taking the house and its visitors back to the frontier.

Florence Bixby, who first lived here in 1906, was responsible for the evolution of the present landscape design, which is distinctive for its several well-defined gardens. Recounting Los Angeles's romantic Spanish past, many of the *rancho*'s gardens are bordered by rough-textured, hand-finished

BELOW LEFT: In the library, a Franciscan tea set, made in Los Angeles, features a delicate Japanese blossom motif. BELOW: In the billiard room, a Mexican *saltillo* from the turn of the century hangs on a wall behind a couch draped with Navajo rugs. A finely inlaid wooden Arabic saddle rests on an arm of the chesterfield. The early-twentieth-century Indian basket is part of the family's collection. Behind the serape curtain, the look changes to Victorian in a bedroom with pale floral wallpaper and fine antiques.

LEFT: The entrance hall, dominated by longhorn steer horns, exhibits the Bixbys' passion for combining many periods and styles. Its western flavor contrasts with the decor in rooms such as the dining room and master bedroom, where cabinets carved by John Bixby, patriarch of the first generation to live here, bring a Victorian influence to the interiors.

RIGHT: Florence Bixby was the first to take charge of landscaping the grounds. In the twenties, she hired a number of well-known plantsmen and designers to assist in developing walks and formal gardens. Although Mrs. Bixby was committed to Mediterranean styles, English garden traditions are also evident. Clipped hedges and perimeter plantings were used to screen and frame sweeping views of surrounding ranchland. BELOW RIGHT: Abel Stearns added a north wing to the original adobe around 1845. Today, its windows are framed with climbing and flowering vines.

ABOVE and FAR RIGHT: Florence Bixby created a very personal "secret garden" where the *rancho's* water tank once stood. She was a private woman who retreated to this small walled garden for seclusion and contemplation, preferring it over the more impressive public spaces, such as the geranium-lined walkway, the rose garden, and the cactus garden. On her trips abroad, Mrs. Bixby bought Della Robbia plaques, decorative tiles, artifacts, and statuary for her gardens, including this reproduction of Praxiteles' "Hercules" (mislabeled "The Faun"). While Mediterranean style dominated the south gardens, other areas were accented with southwestern pots, rugs, and furniture.

walls that evoke old Mexican masonry and are abundant with plantings that are unpretentious and colorful.

Succulents proliferate in the sandy soil of the cactus garden, and herbs thrive in a secluded bed at the south end of the property. A walled secret garden at the west end of the house was Florence's refuge from the world. Here she surrounded herself with decorative tiles and garden art as well as many of her favorite flowers.

In effect, the grounds, steeped in the love of horticulture, are a series of outdoor rooms. Those closest to the house were used for entertaining, and areas farthest for contemplation, horticultural experimentation, and tennis. Connecting the many specialized gardens are walkways delineated by trees and exuberantly flowering vines.

ADOBE LEONIS

A dobe Leonis in Calabasas—L.A.'s horse country—is a reminder of a simpler time. Even though cars on Highway 101 can be seen speeding by in the distance, it's not difficult to imagine the adobe brick structure in the late nineteenth century, when it was the center of a sprawling estate that once spanned much of the west end of the San Fernando Valley and part of Ventura County. Today, the remains of that era include the original house, believed to date back to 1844, a windmill, a pump house, and beautifully maintained gardens and pastures.

For years the property was owned by Miguel Leonis. He was a shrewd and enterprising Basque who made his way to Los Angeles and married an Indian widow, Espíritu Chijulla, heiress to one of three land grants made to Native Americans. Her El Escorpion Rancho was originally part of Mission San Fernando. No one knows who built their adobe, situated by the Calabasas Creek, but in 1880 Leonis extensively expanded and remodeled it in the Monterey style. He paneled the exterior and interior walls with wood and added the distinctive decorative balustrade that runs along the front and sides. For this reason, the house is considered architecturally important, since it represents a transitional style between the simple lines of Monterey and the first suggestions of Victorian gingerbread that would soon sweep through Los Angeles.

Today, Leonis is the oldest of four remaining adobes in the San Fernando Valley. The Leonis Adobe Association maintains the house and property, which sustains livestock similar to what would have been found in Los Angeles before the turn of the century, including Texas longhorn cattle, Cheshire sheep, Guinea hens, and Black Spanish chickens. Craggy cactus gardens still grow in a corner beyond the barn, and wine-producing Mission grapes grow in a small arbor in front of the house.

OPPOSITE: A workroom on the second floor holds mementos from an earlier time. No doubt Miguel and Espíritu Leonis, along with their daughter, Marcellina, hosted many a fandango in their day. Displayed on a wall, along with a violin and a guitar, is a pair of western chaps. None of the rooms had closets, and clothes were typically hung on the walls. **BELOW LEFT:** Orchards and flower beds rim the house and its grounds.

ABOVE: These rare Black Spanish chickens are believed to be the breed that the missionaries first brought with them to California from Spain. Other fowl, including ducks, guineas, turkeys, and pigeons, were raised on the *rancho* and continue to thrive on the property today. **LEFT:** A second-floor veranda overlooks the grape arbor. The *rancho* once encompassed 1100 acres.

PADDISON FARM

FAR LEFT: Only a small parcel remains of the nearly 300-acre farm John Paddison developed in nineteenth-century Norwalk. The fifth generation of Paddison's descendants still live in the house and work the fields, producing corn, grapefruit, avocados, and other vegetables. Indeed, corn shucking and picking contests are still favorite events at parties on the farm. ABOVE: The 1879 Eastlake Victorian farmhouse remains almost in its original state, save for the enclosure of a side porch and the addition of a "modern" kitchen shortly after the 1933 Southern California earthquake.

Development across Los Angeles County has all but erased any vestiges of the booming farm economy that drew trailblazers, entrepreneurs, and vacationers seeking a peaceful and verdant idyll in the nineteenth century. One by one, shopping malls and freeways, office complexes and planned housing communities have taken over where citrus groves and bean fields once flourished.

One family, however, has steadfastly refused to let progress wipe away its precious agricultural legacy. John Paddison, an immigrant from Wales, arrived in the United States in 1869 and, ten years later, bought 46 acres of farmland in Norwalk, which is now an industrial community in southeastern Los Angeles County. There he planted corn, hominy, and alfalfa and started to build his two-story home in the popular Eastlake Victorian style, with decorative

stickwork and an inviting porch. Eventually he increased his land holdings to 300 acres and branched out into dairy farming.

Edward Paddison took over the business following his father's death in 1926. Succumbing to Norwalk's inevitable growth and development, Edward sold off all but six acres. Those acres housed all the original support buildings, which Edward maintained in perfect condition. Still standing on the grounds today are the blacksmith shop, the redwood horse barn, the farmworkers' cottages, the chicken coops, a wash house, a water well, the outhouse, farm equipment, a "modern convenience"—Norwalk's first gasoline pump—and Edward's 1936 Chevrolet flatbed farm truck. Living in the family homestead today are John's great-grandson, Robert Scantlebury, his wife, Margaret, their grown sons, Bobby and Eddie, and a menagerie of family pets, including forty peacocks.

The family lives with the home's original Victorian furnishings and decorative objects, which are enhanced by Margaret's impressive early American quilt collection. Today Paddison Farm is listed on the National Register of Historic Places and is a popular site for romantic weddings and receptions. Not surprisingly, Hollywood film crews gravitate here when seeking to re-create early rural Southern California.

LEFT: The old redwood barn, circa 1879, that houses these chairs and other relics is a visual history of Paddison's past. RIGHT: When Chevrolet needed a Depression-era setting for a 1975 advertisement, the Paddison barn, surrounded by graceful pepper and eucalyptus trees, was painted to fit the scene.

BELOW: Although the grounds of the farm are frequently the site of grand soirees and weddings, the interior of the home is extremely intimate and private. Inside this two-story farmhouse, the Scantlebury family surround themselves with Victorian antiques and scores of family heirlooms. In the master bedroom, the carved-oak bedroom set, which includes this beautiful headboard, was purchased by John Paddison from Sears Roebuck in 1879, when the home was built. Margaret Scantlebury rotates her favorite quilts—including this Grandmother's Garden pattern, at the foot of the bed—among all the beds. The brass and painted-milk-glass chandelier is original to the home.

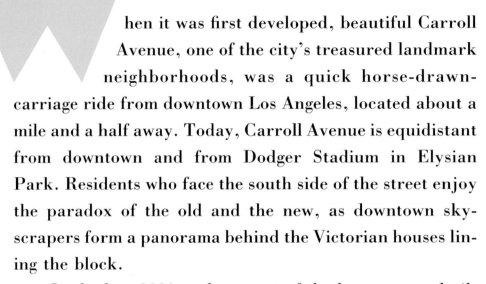

When it was first developed, beautiful Carroll Avenue, one of the city's treasured landmark neighborhoods, was a quick horse-drawn-carriage ride from downtown Los Angeles, located about a mile and a half away. Today, Carroll Avenue is equidistant from downtown and from Dodger Stadium in Elysian Park. Residents who face the south side of the street enjoy the paradox of the old and the new, as downtown skyscrapers form a panorama behind the Victorian houses lining the block.

In the late 1880s, when most of the houses were built on Carroll Avenue, its prosperous inhabitants had moved there to get away from downtown L.A. Shoe magnate Daniel Innes commissioned his house to be built on one of the most prestigious lots on the north side of the street, which even then had a commanding view of the just-developing city. Though his property was no bigger than 50 feet by 100 feet, he had room for his two-story Eastlake Victorian as well as a small barn to house his carriage and horse.

Owner Murray Burns, who now operates the Eastlake Victorian Bed and Breakfast Inn around the corner, bought the Innes House in 1975 and has meticulously restored and furnished it with correct Eastlake details. The colored-glass squares on the bay windows and stair windows are original, as is the massive carved staircase and the built-in fireplace that holds an oil-burning stove in the front parlor. There's nothing timid about the house's deep red exterior, warm gray trims, black sashes, and painted silver accents, all typical of Los Angeles Eastlakes.

LEFT: Entering Innes House through its stained-glass front doors is like taking a step back into turn-of-the-century Los Angeles. Its current owner, Murray Burns, has an educated eye for Victorian detail and has kept the residence true to its era. The very practical exception is that the crystal chandeliers, the brass lamp on the newel post, and the teardrop fixture that hangs in the entry hall would have been powered by gas in their earliest days. **ABOVE:** When this home was built in 1887, Angelenos distinguished their Victorians from San Francisco row houses by putting windows on all four sides of the building, an adaptation made possible by Southern California's affable climate. The result was well-lit interior spaces with refreshing cross-ventilation.

ABOVE: In typical Eastlake Victorian style, the dining room of Innes House is shy of clutter. Under the home's original eyebrow-shaped stained-glass window, a period breakfront displays only a few treasured pieces—the pair of Art Nouveau crystal vases and a small collection of busts, including a French marble sculpture of Joan of Arc. The dining room table and chairs display the narrow bands of shallow geometric carving characteristic of Eastlake furniture. On the table are more Art Nouveau pieces from Burns's collection.

RIGHT: In the main parlor, a velvet settee and matching chairs of Eastlake design are clustered near the fireplace, the slate mantel and cement hearth of which have been marbleized. The vase in the foreground is Austrian Art Nouveau.

ABOVE: Innes House has two parlors adjacent to each other. One, the formal parlor shown in this vignette, was reserved for the most special occasions, such as receiving the minister or making a proposal of marriage. This room could be completely closed off by a sliding door for additional privacy. Here, an Indian brass lamp fringed in crystal stands next to a Greek Revival—style chair that dates from Civil War days. The fireplace features a cherrywood overmantel.

ABOVE: Colorful stained-glass squares like these surrounding the picture window in the formal parlor were often found in Eastlake Victorians.

Bungalow mania hit Los Angeles at the turn of the century.

The Bungalow and Beyond

L.A. was ripe for a new style of architecture. No longer a rustic cow town, it was suddenly a city in search of an identity. Unencumbered by tradition—or by traditional people—the city was open to anything.

2

In 1900, transplants pouring in from points east swelled the population past 100,000, ten times greater than it was at the

LEFT: Although there was nothing modest about this bungalow designed by Arthur S. Heineman in 1909, one-story wood structures like it proliferated in middle-class neighborhoods and were quickly dubbed "California bungalows." TOP RIGHT: *The Craftsman* magazine, published and edited by Gustav Stickley, was the journal that advanced the Arts and Crafts movement throughout the United States. The Craftsman style flourished in the Los Angeles basin, and thousands of simple bungalows with surprisingly creative, hand-finished details were filled with handcrafted furniture and decorative arts. ABOVE RIGHT: Tilemaster Ernest Allan Batchelder had contributed many articles to *The Craftsman* even before he started his own tile company in 1909. An instructor at Harvard Summer School of Design and at Throop

Polytechnic Institute in Pasadena, he espoused the Arts and Crafts doctrine he had studied at the School of Arts and Crafts in Birmingham, England. An enterprising artisan, he fired up his kilns to produce tiles in Pasadena just as the area's housing needs started to swell. Because of his British training, some of his designs featured medieval themes, but many of the most popular had Mayan motifs, like these on the garden wall at his home on the Arroyo in Pasadena (see page 49).

city's centennial in 1881. Newcomers all needed a place to call home—and they needed it fast and cheap.

The bungalow met all of the above conditions, as well as adapting to the climate

and terrain. The bungalow concept is based on the Bengalese native dwelling called a *bangala*, and similar structures have been traced to seventeenth-century Europe. Still, these modest little houses have come to be identified across the country as California bungalows. In its simplest form, a bungalow is a one-story redwood cottage designed for an average American family. Land was inexpensive, and a bungalow could be built for as little as $500 in two months' time. Architects generally were anonymous or otherwise dispensable, since blueprints were readily available from pattern books that sold for a few dollars or were given away by eager real estate speculators. More resourceful types could purchase prefabricated houses, for which the lumber was cut to size and ready to be nailed together.

Entire blocks of these humble bungalows—freestanding or clustered around small courtyards—went up at once. By virtue of sheer numbers, the bungalow be-

LEFT: These two unusual ceramic corbels were cast in 1912 by Ernest Batchelder. He believed that no two tiles should look the same. They are now part of a collection of Batchelder tiles owned by Dr. Robert Winter, who lives in Batchelder's bungalow. RIGHT: On any given day, demolition crews can be spotted razing the city's charming bungalows. Parking lots, strip malls, and apartment buildings often go up in their place.

came the first bona fide residential style of Los Angeles in the twentieth century. By the 1920s, there were tens of thousands of them.

Meanwhile, in late-nineteenth-century England, historian and philosopher John Ruskin and designer William Morris had fathered the Arts and Crafts movement in fierce reaction against the Industrial Revolution. Ruskin proselytized the intrinsic value of handmade goods and the importance of individual expression, while Morris set up a thriving decorative-arts firm, employing a wide spectrum of artisans. In the United States, the message was carried on by Gustav Stickley, a widely copied designer and manufacturer in Syracuse, New York. His Craftsman Workshops produced hand-forged copper utensils, wickerwork, and hand-carved wood furniture, underscoring the involvement of man with his ma-

terials. Stickley's monthly magazine, *The Craftsman*, first published in 1901, spread the word west.

In California, the movement instantly took root. People welcomed a new style that seemed compatible with a love of the outdoors and the informality of their new lives. Californians, in fact, have been credited with creating the widest array of Craftsman houses in the country. They range from the cookie-cutter plainness found in middle-class bungalows to the stylishly sophisticated mansions designed by Northern California architect Bernard Maybeck and Southern California's renowned architectural team Greene and Greene.

In Los Angeles, the beauty of the Craftsman bungalow was that its simple wood form seemed to emerge organically from the earth and its low silhouette didn't disrupt the city's wide-open spaces. Large overhanging eaves created cool, shaded porches for sitting and sleeping. The elimination of narrow hallways allowed spaces to flow into one another and Pacific Ocean breezes to cool the rooms. Each house cried out for its own little garden and a few strategically placed palm trees.

People in California were unconstrained by convention, and their home interiors reflected that. Elaborate Victoriana wouldn't do. Built-in cabinetry, inglenooks, and fireplaces finished in locally fired tiles called for extremely informal furniture. Indian blankets covered the floors, and furniture was sturdy, casual—and inexpensive. A few simple pieces of pottery could be enough to finish a room. The look was consistent with Morris's belief in "works of genuine and beautiful character dedicated rather to the luxury of taste than the luxury of costliness." The extremely popular heavy oak chairs and tables were known around the country as "mission furniture," since the foursquare designs conjured up images of the simple, straightforward structures of the Franciscan padres and also bore a resemblance to the ascetic wooden furniture found in most churches. However, Stickley insisted "mission" was a misnomer and preferred that the style be called simply "Craftsman."

While the period's furniture and decorative arts are now coveted as high-priced antiques, the humble bungalow is at the mercy of the wrecker's ball, destined to be

RIGHT: Charles Sumner Greene and his brother, Henry Mather Greene, employed Mary L. Ranney in their Pasadena architectural firm.

Here, in the foyer of her home (see page 51), their sophisticated aesthetic prevails. The Greenes usually maintained strict design control on homes that bore their stamp, but at this house they made an exception and let Ranney assist in drawing the architectural plans. ABOVE: Today, the home's owners, David and Judith Brown, have respected the Greenes' Asian sensibility, as seen here in the bedroom. American antiques blend with the futon and obi-silk pillows. BELOW RIGHT: A reproduction of a Greene and Greene lantern lights the way to the front door of the Ranney House.

replaced by huge condominium buildings and apartment complexes in many Los Angeles communities. It's a rare neighborhood—such as parts of Pasadena, Hollywood, Venice, Santa Monica, and the West Adams district in Central L.A.—where the bungalows' simple, rustic qualities are appreciated by middle-income homeowners, the very people for whom they were originally intended.

In its most elaborate form, the bungalow could be as elegant as a two-story mansion with servants' quarters, Tiffany glass windows, and exquisitely finished mahogany, ebony, and teakwood detailing. Cincinnati-born brothers Charles Sumner Greene and Henry Mather Greene per-

RIGHT: Broad overhang-
ing eaves are dominant
features of the Gamble
House, a mansionlike
bungalow designed by
Greene and Greene. The
extended roofline keeps
the sun at bay and cre-
ates shaded terraces
and sleeping porches. In
addition, the sweeping
horizontal lines visu-
ally integrate the house
with the land it
occupies.

fected this form, creating Craftsman houses that became monuments to Southern California idealism.

After training at the Massachusetts Institute of Technology, the Greenes arrived in the resort community of Pasadena, the former Rancho San Pascual. Located a few miles north of L.A.'s downtown, the town was nicknamed "the Indiana Colony" for its large contingent of transplanted Midwesterners. En route to join their parents, who sought better health in Southern California, the brothers stopped at the 1893 World's Columbian Exhibition in Chicago. There they were awed by Ho-o-den, a half-size replica of a Buddhist temple, which was their introduction to the Japanese aesthetic. Their friendship with a Pasadena Asian antiques dealer, John Bentz, furthered their knowledge of Japanese architecture. In 1906, the house they designed for Bentz on Prospect Boulevard (a street that welcomes visitors with Greene and Greene stone gateposts) became a labora-

ABOVE LEFT: The Gamble House was the ultimate bungalow, but most Los Angeles bungalows were built on a smaller scale. On Sherman Canal in Venice, a rickety picket fence surrounds Martin Gardner's tiny gray house, with its fuchsia door and a pair of towering palms. BELOW RIGHT: The Hollywood Hills frame one of many blocks of bungalows. Unlike the cookie-cutter housing tracts built in Los Angeles today, no two bungalows look the same, yet the low profile they share unifies the neighborhood.

tory for their future designs and remains today in almost perfect condition.

In a short time, the Greenes would merge nuances of Japanese architecture with American Shingle and Swiss-chalet influences to create several stunning examples of their particular version of Craftsman style. The houses were linear and clean yet undeniably ornamental. In their hands, ordinary elements such as drainage pipes and pegged carpentry joints were elevated to art forms. Every lighting fixture and piece of furniture bore their stamp.

Unlike the bungalows designed for Everyman, the Greenes' so-called ultimate bungalows could only be enjoyed by

wealthy patrons. Although they also built homes in Northern California, their commissions from wealthy families in Pasadena are regarded as their finest works. The Robert Blacker House on Hillcrest Avenue (1907) remains one of the city's most spectacular residences, a sprawling three-story structure with a dramatic porte cochere and harmonious Japanese gardens. A subsequent owner sold off the Greene and Greene fixtures and subdivided the property, but it is currently being restored to its original elegance.

The showpiece Gamble House (1908) was designed and built for Procter & Gamble heir David Gamble of Cincinnati when he and his wife Mary retired and bought land on Westmoreland Place. The mansion is a treasury of Greene and Greene artistry, from the carpeting to the wooden picture frames to the Tiffany glass lanterns, windows, and doors. Bequeathed by the Gamble family to the City of Pasadena and the University of Southern California School of Architecture and Fine Arts, the house today is open to the public as a museum. Other architects who put their imprint on Craftsman-style homes in the area included Arthur and Alfred Heineman, Frederick Roehrig, Sumner P. Hunt, Louis du Puget Millar, Louis B. Easton, and G. Lawrence Stimson.

While Pasadena attracted its share of wealthy industrialists who built expensive homes and belonged to the exclusive Valley Hunt Club, it was also home to a thriving artists' colony known as the Arroyo Culture. This group got its name from the beautiful Arroyo Seco, a boulder-encrusted dry gulch that channeled through Pasadena, and separated city from wilderness and high society from bohemia. Lining the ridge above the Arroyo were small bungalows inhabited by artists and intellectuals, who surrounded themselves with tiles, pottery, and other decorative arts produced

BELOW: Although *Arroyo Craftsman* magazine lasted for only one issue, the Craftsman aesthetic it glorified still thrives today.

locally. With a communal spirit, many artists joined forces to form the short-lived Arroyo Guild of Craftsmen, and even published, albeit only for one issue (October 1909), *Arroyo Craftsman* magazine.

However transitory, the Arroyo Culture represented a dedicated and sincere effort to further the Craftsman ethic, and its members left their mark on Los Angeles. Painter William Lees Judson founded the School of Fine Arts, which eventually became the College of Fine Arts at the University of Southern California. Chicagoan-turned-Pasadenan Amos G. Throop established Throop Polytechnic Institute, the forerunner to the California Institute of Technology. One of the founders of the Arroyo Culture, Charles Fletcher Lummis, city editor of the *Los Angeles Times*, had built his own house, El Alisal, with Arroyo boulders; he also founded the Southwest Museum, which today houses one of the finest collections of American Indian art. His California Landmarks Club, founded in 1895 to achieve the restoration of the missions, had a powerful impact on the architecture of the city over the next century.

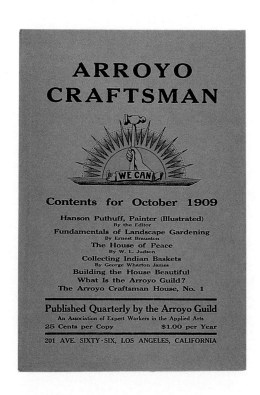

ARROYO
CRAFTSMAN

WE CAN

Contents for October 1909

Hanson Puthuff, Painter (Illustrated)
By the Editor
Fundamentals of Landscape Gardening
By Ernest Braunton
The House of Peace
By W. L. Judson
Collecting Indian Baskets
By George Wharton James
Building the House Beautiful
What Is the Arroyo Guild?
The Arroyo Craftsman House, No. 1

Published Quarterly by the Arroyo Guild
An Association of Expert Workers in the Applied Arts
25 Cents per Copy $1.00 per Year
201 AVE. SIXTY-SIX, LOS ANGELES, CALIFORNIA

BATCHELDER HOUSE

LEFT: Entering the front door of Batchelder House in Pasadena, guests are struck by the art-glass inset in the hand-forged copper doorplate. BELOW: The walls and floor of the breakfast nook are tiled with Batchelder's trademark matte-finish ceramic tiles, all in the quiet earthy palette so typical of the Arts and Crafts style. BELOW RIGHT: In the living room, the fireplace reaches to the rafters

harp, to honor her musical spirit. On the right, another lion holds Batchelder's personal crest, the hare as artist, a motif taken from the English Arts and Crafts movement. On the ledge is a lamp by Dirk van Erp, of Oakland and San Francisco. ABOVE RIGHT: The glorified bungalow, with its second-story bedrooms, features redwood shingles and an Arroyo boulder chimney that have weathered gracefully.

and is the pièce de résistance of the house. Batchelder designed it as a wedding present for his beloved wife, Alice. Inlaid on the left is a tile showing a lion holding a crest of a

The Ernest A. Batchelder house is nestled under towering oak trees on the edge of Pasadena's rustic Arroyo Seco. A charming tile path leads to the hand-hewn Craftsman bungalow, with its second-floor sleeping porch. It was behind this Swiss-chalet-inspired house that Batchelder set up his kiln and practiced the art of decorative tile work. His range of designs spanned from Aztec- and Mayan-inspired patterns to Italian, Byzantine, Spanish Colonial, and art deco motifs. Among the greatest showpieces of Batchelder tile are the lobby of the Fine Arts Building in downtown Los Angeles, Chicago's Union Station, and the Maritime Building in Vancouver. Despite a thriving business in the first decades of the twentieth century, Batchelder's tile works faltered during the Depression and he was forced to turn off his kiln.

The house he built for himself and his wife, Alice Coleman, a pianist, is a monument to his artistry. While Batchelder tile fireplace surrounds were a popular fixture in homes built throughout Southern California in the years between 1910 and 1932, his own home displays his work at every turn.

Robert Winter, the current owner and an architectural historian at nearby Occidental College, has painstakingly rekindled the Craftsman spirit. Arts and Crafts furniture, pottery and glass, and paintings from the California Plein Air impressionist school reflect his deep understanding of Batchelder's aesthetic.

RANNEY HOUSE

I n 1907, because of the popularity of Charles and Henry Greene's Craftsman designs and the resulting increase in commissions, the brothers decided to expand their firm. It was around then that Mary L. Ranney joined the firm as a draftsman, although several years later she went on to found Pasadena's Westridge School for Girls. Her first residential project was assisting in the design and construction of her own home, a two-story shingled structure with Oriental overtones. Built in 1907, it is located on the prominent corner of Orange Grove Boulevard and Arroyo Terrace in a neighborhood that has become a mecca for architectural historians. The tree-lined streets in that area house a total of eight Greene and Greene houses, including the famous Gamble House.

LEFT: David and Judith Brown quickly recognized that Ranney House, an early-twentieth-century design by Charles and Henry Greene, is the ideal setting for two large sculptural Akari paper lanterns designed by Los Angeles native Isamu Noguchi. The Greene brothers had been greatly influenced by traditional Japanese architecture. Here, the sparely furnished living room with its bands of teak is viewed from the main entry hall. RIGHT: Hand-split redwood-shingle siding sheathes the exterior walls. A clinker brick wall fronts the porch, where a new red-toned teak door has replaced the original.

Although it is one of the Greenes' more reserved plans, the Ranney House remains one of their most inviting. Its front porch is distinguished by a low clinker brick wall that leads to a paneled teak-and-white-pine door with seed-glass insets. Inside, the Greenes' sophisticated cabinetry, horizontal bands of polished Burmese teak, and pegged scarf joints are recurring motifs.

After years of neglect, the Ranney House was meticulously restored in the 1980s. Contemporary artisans recreated the Greenes' custom-designed mahogany lighting fixtures, which they suspended from leather straps, and

glass cabinets were built on both sides of the tiled fireplace. The home is now owned by David and Judith Brown, whose collections of Japanese ceramics and Noguchi paper lanterns perfectly suit the house's Asian aesthetic. The couple has shied away from the typically massive Arts and Crafts furniture that is usually found in Greene and Greene houses. Instead, they have combined International Style, Shaker, and modern Craftsman pieces to create a refreshingly contemporary atmosphere. The enclosed sleeping porches, so typical of early-twentieth-century California bungalows, have become recreation areas for the Browns' three young children. In the rear garden, a new pool and hot tub have been artfully designed to meld with the simple Japanese landscape originally planned by the Greene brothers. Blooming pink camellias and azaleas harmonize with the bungalow's weathered gray-green redwood shingles.

FAR LEFT: A newly executed Arts and Crafts– style table and chairs work in concert with the highly refined architectural scheme of the wood-paneled dining room. Overhead is a chandelier made recently for the house in the spirit of Greene and Greene. LEFT, MIDDLE: On a contemporary black table, Japanese boxes and red lacquer bowls, contemporary American pottery, and a Noguchi lamp create a serene still life. LEFT: New cabinetry, containing iridescent stained- glass light boxes, was installed around the fireplace. On the mantel above the earth-colored tile fireplace is a stack of new Shaker boxes and a portrait of Sitting Bull by Los Angeles artist Salomon Huerta. **ABOVE: A teak-framed window in the kitchen allows a view into a small breakfast room. The classic modern furnishings, including an Alvar Aalto table and three stacking stools, blend seamlessly with the house's Asian aesthetic. In the adjoining living room is a brown leather chair by Marcel Breuer.**

RYAN / ROCHE HOUSE

The surprise of this house is that its Craftsman interior is so unlike its Mediterranean Revival façade. The two-story stucco house features thirteen pairs of pillars that support the balcony and form the porte cochere—a high-style façade in 1911.

Developers Daniel T. and John Althouse built the house in a newly developing suburb west of downtown L.A. that was accessible by electric train. Near the Los Angeles Country Club and the original Harvard School for Boys, the neighborhood was attractive to upper-middle-class professionals and entrepreneurs. They considered the move west rather daring, considering that the hub of most residential neighborhoods was still closer to downtown.

The Ryan/Roche house was one of five Althouse residences in the suburb; the exteriors of the others were more consistent with the prevailing Arts and Crafts mode. It is believed that artisans working for Greene and Greene were employed to craft the superior woodwork that appears throughout the house. Details such as ebony pegs on the fireplace corbels and bookcase doors with an inverted "cloud lift" motif were unmistakable signatures of the Greene brothers.

The house's current owners, Joe Ryan and Charles Roche, came to the rescue of this aging Craftsman marvel and restored it faithfully and completely in 1990. The fur-

LEFT: Simple but sturdy Craftsman furniture and pottery create a pleasing composition in the sunny breakfast room of Joe Ryan and Charles Roche's period house. The oak rocker behind the wicker table was crafted by L. and J. G. Stickley. On the mahogany side table, birds of paradise arranged in a ringed Bauer vase stand next to a Weller pitcher. Resting against the wall is a hammered copper tray of the same era. The bowl on the lower shelf of the wicker table is by Van Briggle Pottery of Colorado Springs, Colorado. The blue glass-and-copper lighting fixture, with its silhouetted Dutch scene, is original to the house. ABOVE: One of Los Angeles's ubiquitous palm trees grows front and center at this Mediterranean Revival house.

nishings and decorative arts they added are among the finest examples of America's Arts and Crafts period.

The only departure from the original plans is the state-of-the-art kitchen, complete with new mahogany cabinets, which exists in perfect harmony with the rest of the home.

ABOVE: Drapes of iridescent taffeta and walls covered in French silk velvet add a touch of old-world luxury to the living room. Surrounding the fireplace are tiles thought to be made by Grueby of Boston. The small wooden table in front of the sofa is by Roycroft and supports a candleholder by Gustav Stickley. The copper lamp in the foreground was designed by Dirk van Erp. The chair in the foreground and the library table are by Charles P. Limbert. The chair in the background is by L. and J. G. Stickley. **LEFT:** The mahogany breakfront features unusual beveled leaded-glass panels with a water lily motif. The dining-room chairs were designed by Gustav Stickley, and all the ceramic pieces are by Rookwood Pottery of Cincinnati, Ohio. The frieze bordering the room is stenciled canvas.

LEFT: The new kitchen is a veritable showcase of rare Arts and Crafts pottery. The glass and mahogany cupboards house pieces by Van Briggle, Hampshire, Weller, the University of North Dakota School of Mines, and the Fulper Pottery Company of Flemington, New Jersey. The vase on the granite counter is also from the Fulper kilns. The lighting fixture near the door is an outdoor lantern from the period.

RIGHT: Fine Arts and Crafts furniture and Navajo rugs are arranged in this bedroom and the adjoining sunroom. The quarter-sawn oak bed is typical of the period. The finest Craftsman artisans used quarter-sawn oak for its treasured vertical grain lines, achieved by cutting the wood against the grain. The quilt was made in Yakima, Washington, by Roche's mother, Amy. BELOW: On the top shelves of the Charles P. Limbert china cabinet next to the bed are a pair of lanterns that were originally part of a dance hall in Illinois. The Fulper vase stands above a Swiss cowbell dated 1878. On the wall are hand-tinted photographs of national parks that were originally sold as souvenirs. The oak mantel clock is also from the Craftsman period.

RIGHT: The mahogany-paneled entry hall is lit with a silver-plate and crystal chandelier that was installed by the builder of the house. An Arts and Crafts lamp and a small vase from Grueby Pottery sit atop a mahogany Craftsman table. The top of the "gentleman caller's bench" is hinged to provide storage and is covered with a 1920s Navajo blanket and pillows made from remnants of Oriental carpets.

HARBY HOUSE

The Craftsman style is timeless. It works as well now that the century is reaching its close as it did when the century began. This modern Craftsman house blends with other period bungalows in a Santa Monica neighborhood. It is the comfortable home of Stephen Harby, an architect who moved to Southern California in 1977 from Cambridge, Massachusetts, to work as an associate with Moore Ruble Yudell Architects and Planners. "Craftsman architecture is the most interesting indigenous style here, and not just the famous Greene and Greene houses," says Harby, who designed the remodel of a tiny bungalow, expanding it into this duplex in 1991 with his colleague, James Morton, and with Dani Rosen.

Unlike the earliest Craftsman houses, in which the wood was left unpainted, Harby's house is colorful, with green walls inside and out. The ceilings are two shades of

pale gray in the living room and light blue and green in the dining room. The master bedroom walls are rose, accented with the ubiquitous green.

Latticework trellises enclose the front porch and are covered with young wisteria vines. When the vines are mature, the vibrant purple flowers and green leaves will enclose the space and the porch will become the first "room" visitors enter. Another outdoor room, a large central patio, adjoins the living room and breakfast room via several sets of double doors.

In the Craftsman tradition, much of the furniture is built-in. Aside from some antique pieces, most of the freestanding furniture was designed by Harby and executed by Santa Barbara wood craftsman Alphonse Franssen, who also did the complex carpentry in the house.

FAR LEFT: In the breakfast room, a classic American table and Mexican iron chairs from the 1940s are positioned on a Turkish kilim rug. Harby designed the wooden light sconce. **LEFT:** The mahogany dining-room table is set with Harby family English bone china. On the mantel over the brick fireplace is an heirloom New Haven clock. A pair of brass candlesticks flank a print of fifteenth-century Venice. **ABOVE:** Centered under the sky-blue and green tray ceiling, six oak office chairs provide comfortable seating. The unglazed terra-cotta figure on the bookshelf is from Oaxaca in southern Mexico. The dining room is adjacent to a hall library that stores Harby's collection of architecture tomes.

LEFT: The breakfast room serves as the central room of the house. All other public rooms, as well as the main oak staircase, which leads to the master bedroom and Harby's home office, radiate from it. Above the pine love seat is a pencil drawing of an Istanbul interior by the Venice Beach artist Stephen Sidelinger.

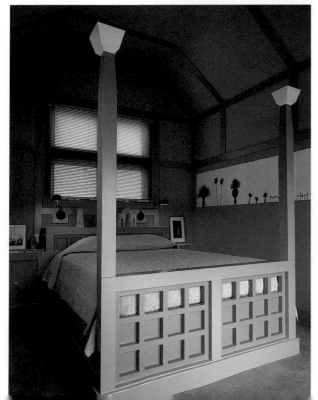

LEFT: The walls and barnlike vaulted ceiling of the master bedroom are painted a subdued shade of rose and accented with a soft green. Harby designed the lattice pattern on the headboard and footboard of the four-poster bed to repeat the pattern on the balcony it faces. The portraits of neighborhood palms are by Sidelinger. ABOVE: Another sculpture by William Harby and an heirloom clock grace the cabinet in the breakfast room, near the entrance to the kitchen. To the left of the door is a drawing by British artist Glynn Boyde-Harte, and to the right are three gouaches from Harby's Sidelinger collection. In the compact kitchen, emerald-green tiles provide a refreshing jolt of color.

Perhaps because Los Angeles came of age in the twentieth century, its need

Reconnecting with the Past

for roots is extremely strong. Along with the urge to be unconventional, Angelenos have always craved a sense of place and history, even if they had to create it themselves.

To affirm their own cultural heritage, and perhaps prove something to the rest of the country, which often deems Los Angeles a cultural wasteland, people in the city have grasped at fragments

LEFT: Crowds congregated before the open pipe organ at the Panama-California Exposition of 1915 in San Diego's Balboa Park. The opulent Spanish architecture of the exhibition buildings ushered in an era of architectural preoccupation with Mediterranean forms, known as the Spanish Colonial Revival, which endures to this day. ABOVE: The image of a brown bear, the symbol of California that appears on the state flag, is rendered in stained glass in a window at La Casa Nueva, one of the grandest Spanish Colonial Revival houses in Los Angeles, built by oil tycoon Walter P. Temple. Construction of the house began in 1919, and it now can be seen on the grounds of the Workman and Temple Family Homestead in the City of Industry. **RIGHT: Although fruit groves have virtually disappeared from the urban landscape, trees bearing plump grapefruits and other citrus varieties continue to be a familiar sight in residential gardens, both large and small.**

of the past. That explains why Taco Bell stands look like cartoon versions of Franciscan missions and why upscale new tract communities are stamped out in earth-colored stucco and red tile roofs.

The past here means different things to different people. It may be as faint as a rustic wood-frame cabin in Santa Monica Canyon that suggests a bit of the old frontier, or a priceless collection of Navajo rugs in a Century City townhouse that fulfills an unconscious yearning for the simple life the West has always symbolized.

In other major cities, historic buildings are an accessible source of tradition,

but in Los Angeles those sources had to be invented. By the turn of the century, the missions were in ruins and the adobes of El Pueblo had for the most part been razed.

Nevertheless, before World War I ended, the city was ready to reconnect with whatever memories it could find. One way was to invent its own lore and architectural vocabulary.

Starting in 1920, a second population explosion brought an influx of new Californians—more than 1.2 million, many of whom arrived in their own cars on newly constructed national highways. For many, the attraction was economic: money could be made in the land boom that caused new towns to crop up overnight. The new port of Los Angeles and the opening of the Panama Canal in 1914 were transforming the city into a world trade center with a major

TOP: The novel *Ramona*, by Helen Hunt Jackson, a best-selling romance set in mission days, kindled a dreamy interest in the region's Spanish past. The nineteen-year-old heroine, Ramona Ortegna, is a half-Indian orphan raised as Spanish, whose love for an Indian man has dire consequences. *Ramona* fever lasted into the thirties. ABOVE: In the courtyard of the Spanish-Mexican-style house owned by Roger Simon (see page 99), a tiled mural depicts Mexican vaqueros roping steer.

shipping business. And the burgeoning oil and film industries were glamorous new fields that provided jobs for legions. In 1926, the motion-picture business was one of the state's top moneymakers and the fourth-largest industry in the world.

By decade's end, when the Depression hit, carloads of families continued to migrate west. The region offered an escape from the dismal conditions in other parts of the country. When they arrived, newcomers found Los Angeles in the midst of a depression too. But warm weather made the hard times more tolerable—Los Angeles was a place where people could plant their hopes and start anew.

Thrust into a world where little was familiar, these new transplants longed for a bit of established culture to embrace. The pure and simple legends of California's Spanish past evidently provided meaning for them, for its manifestations would become—and remain—the vernacular architecture of Los Angeles.

The single cultural event that ignited a widespread infatuation with Spanish architecture was the opening of the Panama-California Exposition of 1915 in San Diego. Bertram Grosvenor Goodhue, working with Carleton M. Winslow, Sr., designed the buildings for the fair resurrecting the exuberantly ornamental Churrigueresque Spanish style. The pièce de résistance was the California State Building, now the Museum of Man in San Diego's Balboa Park. Although the look, and the movement that ensued, became identified as Spanish Colonial Revival, its likes had never been seen in California until then.

The fair's impact, coupled with enthusiasm for earlier examples of Spanish buildings from as far back as 1900, created a vogue for all manner of housing in the Spanish tradition that reached its apex during the 1920s and the early 1930s. The Spanish Colonial Revival style was some-

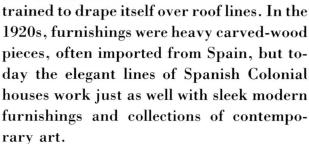

times referred to as Mediterranean Revival, a broad term that alluded to the region's Spanish, Italian, and North African influences as well as to the city's temperate climate. Mediterranean Revival worked as well for formal houses and large rambling hillside estates as it did for informal, tiny tract houses. So quickly adopted were its forms that the look also became known as California Spanish, California Colonial, or simply Californian.

The style is still characterized by smooth stucco walls, low-pitched red tile roofs, lyrical iron gates, window grates, and balconies. Colorful tiles enliven fireplaces, stair risers, and floors. Equally important are patios, courtyards, and lush gardens planted with fruit trees—orange, lemon, grapefruit, apricot, plum, fig, avocado—palm trees, and rolling green lawns. Adding the final burst of color is bougainvillea in vibrant shades of orange, purple, and pink, which frequently is

ABOVE: L.A.-booster Charles Lummis filled his home, El Alisal, or "place of the sycamore," with a profusion of books, photographs, and Native American baskets, pottery, and textiles, which are now assembled at the nearby Southwest Museum, founded by Lummis in 1907. ABOVE RIGHT: Lummis's Mission Revival house reflected his interest in preserving the California missions. He built it of boulders from the neighboring Arroyo Seco. Today it is a State Historical Monument and the headquarters of the Historical Society of Southern California. BELOW LEFT: Charles Lummis immersed himself in American Indian and Hispanic culture. Despite his carriage-trade background, he often wore a sombrero and corduroys.

trained to drape itself over roof lines. In the 1920s, furnishings were heavy carved-wood pieces, often imported from Spain, but today the elegant lines of Spanish Colonial houses work just as well with sleek modern furnishings and collections of contemporary art.

Being true to history was never as important as being picturesque when it came to the L.A. version of Spanish architecture. When the mood hit them, architects borrowed liberally from the Middle East, North Africa, and Italy as well as from the missions, Monterey style, and Mexican adobes.

It was inevitable that fantasy would play a considerable role too. The city was maturing along with the film industry, and architects were building manors for movie stars and movie moguls. For Hollywood's royalty, it was important that their homes be as glamorous as their images. Wallace Neff, Southern California's preeminent residential Spanish Colonial Revivalist, was the darling of the movie set, having received commissions from Joan Bennett, Charles Chaplin, Darryl Zanuck, and King Vidor. (The famous Pickfair estate he redesigned for Mary Pickford and Douglas Fairbanks

Mission Inn Riverside, Calif.

wasn't Spanish at all, but English Regency—see pages 226–227.) Neff took liberties with tradition by creating a sense of drama. He turned straight lines into graceful curves, adding imaginative elliptical arches and curving staircases. He willingly obliged when a client wanted kitsch, such as the ersatz coat of arms he created for the entrance of the Beverly Hills estate of scriptwriter Frances Marion and her husband, cowboy star Fred Thomson.

While Neff was satisfying the whims of Hollywood's newly moneyed, architects Myron Hunt and Elmer Grey were designing many of the region's landmarks, including the First Congregational Church in Riverside, the campuses of Throop Institute of Technology (later the venerated California Institute of Technology), Pomona College in Claremont, and Occidental College in Los Angeles, and the estates for banker G. W. Wattles in Hollywood and railroad magnate Henry Huntington in San Marino, both now open to the public. Working alone, Hunt built the Rose Bowl Stadium and the legendary Ambassador Hotel.

Other Spanish Colonial Revival architects whose work left an imprint on the city included Santa Monica's John W. Byers; Pasadena's Gordon Kaufmann, Roland E. Coate, and Reginald Johnson; and Santa Barbara's George Washington Smith. San Francisco's Julia Morgan, the architect of William Randolph Hearst's castle at San Simeon, designed Hearst's *Los*

ABOVE: The printed message on the back of a postcard from the Mission Inn reads, in part, that it is "the one hotel which a Californian can recognize as his own." BELOW: Charles Lummis edited the magazine *Land of Sunshine* to promote tourism here. He enlisted many sympathetic East Coast writers to fill its pages.

Angeles Herald Examiner headquarters in downtown Los Angeles as well as several other buildings in the area.

A look back even further into Los Angeles history shows that before the turn of the century Angelenos were yearning to link up with the past.

Charles Fletcher Lummis was a flamboyant newspaperman-cum-philosopher who almost single-handedly invented a mythology of Los Angeles that would continue to draw tourists here for a hundred years. Lummis was drawn here in part by the phenomenally popular novel *Ramona*, written by Helen Hunt Jackson in 1884, which glorified life in the missions and *ranchos* of early California. Lummis walked from his home in Cincinnati to Los Angeles, a journey that kindled his fascination with Native American culture. He chronicled the trip, especially his experiences with Southwestern Indian tribes, for the *Los Angeles Times*, where he was hired as the paper's first city editor upon his arrival. Later this promotion-minded graduate of Harvard University became editor of *Land of Sunshine*, later known as *Out West*, a magazine designed to extol the West and encourage tourism. Through his voluminous writings, Lummis became the city's most outspoken supporter, unraveling a legend of the missions and the West that the Indians and padres probably would never have recognized but that nevertheless captured the hearts of the country.

Lummis observed that "Plymouth Rock was a state of mind. So were the California missions," and he became determined to preserve them. The mission buildings had been abandoned for fifty years when Lummis led a campaign to restore them. His California Landmarks Club was one of America's first preservationist organizations. Based on the millions of tourist dollars that mission lore generated, Lummis determined that the mission structures were, indeed, next to the climate, "the best capital Southern California has." He was so zealous about these shrines to the city's Spanish past that he spent twelve years building his own home in homage to his beloved sanctuaries, complete with bell tower and the obligatory archways. Many cite his house, El Alisal, as the first Mission Revival structure in Los Angeles, a particularly significant citation because Lummis was not an architect.

But the Mission movement was in the air. At about the same time that Lummis was hauling out boulders from the Arroyo Seco to build the walls of his house, U.S. Senator Leland Stanford, railroad mogul and former California governor, was thinking about the missions too. In 1886, he commissioned the Boston architectural firm Shepley, Rutan and Coolidge to design buildings for Stanford University in the Northern California community of Palo Alto. When Stanford demanded a design that reflected California's past, the architects' solution was low, arched, and arcaded stone structures surrounding patios and plazas.

Buildings with an ecclesiastical feel started to surface throughout California as early as the 1890s. They were distinguished by unadorned planes of white stucco, rounded parapets, arched entrances, quatrefoil windows, low-pitched tile roofs, and even modified *campanarios* and bell towers. Architectural references to the missions were the rage from 1900 to 1915 and again in the 1930s. On a drive from downtown to the ocean along Sunset Boulevard, tourists could see gas stations, schools, apartments, houses, and Elmer Grey's still impressive Beverly Hills Hotel, all vaguely evoking Padre Junípero Serra's vision. Near Los Angeles in Riverside, a huge hotel called the Mission Inn was the Disneyland of its day, attracting more tourists than the missions themselves. Elaborate in detail,

BELOW: The myth of the West dominates many Angelenos' lives today. Here, in the "clubhouse" behind their demure Tudor home, Robert and Rhonda Heintz spend their leisure hours surrounded by hay bales, Indian blankets, and rustic cabin furniture. The Heintzes have developed a business out of dealing in such flea-market collectibles. ABOVE RIGHT: Mementos such as vintage cowboy gauntlets are among the prizes to be found at these markets, along with well-worn spurs, saddles, and boots. RIGHT: Architectural authenticity is rarely as important as the spirit that goes into a look. The Heintzes' clubhouse is in fact a one-time rabbit hutch, with three walls and a slant roof. It has been fully furnished and comes complete with TV set and hickory dining table.

with scalloped, parapeted gables and decorative domes, it was the most overdone yet most publicized example of the mythologized Mission style.

Ironically, it was the unpretentious lines of the original missions that led to some of California's most avant-garde architecture. With more ingenuity and restraint than theatrical gewgaws, a streamlined version of Mission Revival emerged from the drawing board of Irving Gill. A contemporary of Frank Lloyd Wright, the forward-thinking Gill eschewed wood in favor of concrete, a medium he likened to adobe, and trimmed his design elements to a functional few—the straight line, the arch, the cube, and the circle. His modernist thinking predated the international modern movement that reached Los Angeles in the 1920s.

LEFT: This simple, una-
dorned house, part of a
small colony of archi-
tecturally unique adobe
bungalows, is reminis-
cent of the Old Califor-
nia buildings that
inspired its architect,
Carleton Winslow, Sr.,
in the early twentieth

ADOBE COLONY

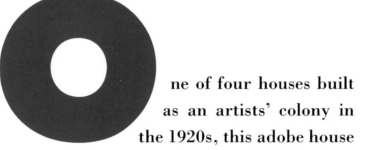

century. The streetside
façade, with its rough-
hewn walls, is punc-
tuated with narrow
windows protected with
hand-turned wood

grates. A wrought-iron
Mexican lantern illumi-
nates the front en-
trance. Drought-
tolerant plants fill the
garden bed. ABOVE: Be-
fore entering the house
itself, visitors must pass
through a heavy wood
gate that opens onto the
courtyard of this latter-
day adobe structure.
BELOW LEFT: Outlining
the property is an un-
dulating wall, given
character by its faded
and chipped paint. Visi-
tors to the tranquillity
found herein pass
through a time warp
between the sounds and
sights of ultra-urban
Southern California and
this 1920s relic.

O ne of four houses built as an artists' colony in the 1920s, this adobe house was designed by Spanish Colonial Revivalist architect Carleton Winslow, Sr. (who had assisted Bertram Goodhue on the monumental downtown Los Angeles Public Library project, begun in 1922). The house is one of the few surviving examples of adobe structures built in Southern California in the twentieth century. Winslow, who had restored the nineteenth-century Adobe Flores nearby, clearly modeled this house after early California dwellings. The thick, whitewashed adobe walls insulate as efficiently for the current owner as any modern air-conditioning system, and its two fireplaces quickly warm the entire house in winter. Furnished with European and Oriental furniture and antiques and a fine portrait collection dating from the

seventeenth through the nineteenth century, the house recreates the ambiance of one of its nineteenth-century Mexican predecessors. The adobe surrounds a charming tiled patio that welcomes the afternoon sun.

LEFT: An intricately carved mahogany sideboard, along with other furnishings that belonged to the owner's mother, give the dining room a European sensibility. Family crystal and silver are proudly displayed. At teatime, the heirlooms sparkle, especially when light bounces off grape-cluster shade pulls made of Bavarian glass. Grapevines also figure in the stained-glass work reflected in the gilt-framed mirror. BELOW: A shady corner of the courtyard is a cool refuge when temperatures rise in Southern California. BELOW RIGHT: As viewed through a rustic peephole, lush greenery accents a small shrine made of redwood near the front entrance. RIGHT: In an office nook, a Spanish carved-wood Saint Anne statue that once graced a church now stands on the hearth of a beehive fireplace. Next to the figure, an arched picture window, its mullions doubling as shelves, supports potted violets and a collection of angels silhouetted against the light.

ZANE GREY PUEBLO HOUSE

For all the architectural revivals that Los Angeles spawned—including Spanish, English, French, even Egyptian—the one that had trouble taking hold was the Pueblo Revival. Historically, the difficulty makes sense, since the indigenous Gabrielino Indians themselves never built pueblos. Instead, the Gabrielinos lived in wickiups, thatch structures made of fern and tule, hardly a design destined to catch on.

It took a passionate lover of the Southwest to build this striking pueblo in the Altadena foothills beneath the majestic San Gabriel Mountains. In 1928, Zane Grey, the writer of western fiction and author of *Riders of the Purple Sage*, built the house for his wife's first cousin, who was his secretary, illustrator, and constant traveling companion, Mildred Smith.

Grey commissioned noted Los Angeles Spanish Revivalist Elmer Grey (no relation) to construct the house, in which no opportunity to restate the Indian theme was overlooked. For the tiled grand staircase, Pasadena tile maker Ernest Batchelder incorporated images of pre-Columbian gods. Thunderbird motifs appeared on wrought-iron wall sconces. Perhaps the most original detail can be found in the large study on the second floor. There, Indian baskets —two Navajo, one Apache—were inverted and used as hanging lamps.

The current owners have maintained the integrity of the architecture and added their own collections of Native American handicrafts and rugs, along with African baskets and colorful Pendleton blankets.

LEFT: The grand staircase of this home, commissioned by western writer Zane Grey, is draped with a dramatic garland of magnolia branches. The tiled stairs, which are in pristine condition, are prized for their unusual display of earth-toned tower over it, and, along one side, an Australian tea tree grows. **TOP RIGHT: In the study upstairs, with its hanging lights made of Indian baskets, the current owners celebrate the region as well. They have incorporated Pendleton blan-**

Batchelder designs depicting pre-Columbian gods. Watching over the stairway is a terracotta Mexican angel. The chair is Dutch. ABOVE: This Pueblo or Hopi Revival house reflects the author's affection for the West and Southwest. Palm trees kets, Navajo rugs, and contemporary Mexican furniture into the scheme, along with their collections of African baskets and Skookum dolls from the thirties, forties, and fifties. Above the mantel is a Charles M. Russell print.

PORTER FARMHOUSE

FAR LEFT: Shirley and Peter Porter's provincial home, tucked behind layers of shrubs, trees, and dormant climbing vines, is a serene counterpoint to the bustle of the city. Romantic balconies provide unobstructed views of the property, while a meandering curb, fashioned from boulders unearthed from the nearby Arroyo Seco riverbed, adds natural texture. **LEFT:** On a plain white wall under a balcony, a makeshift arrangement of a crude folk-art crucifix and a rusting iron horse creates an intriguing vignette.

O n a small bend in a rustic road in Pasadena, there is an intimate cluster of houses that instantly evokes feelings of pastoral Spain—a Spain that existed only in the imagination of its builder. Architectural designer Edward Fowler, who was said to be inspired by magazine illustrations, is credited with 1300 houses. In the 1920s, at the height of Los Angeles's Spanish Colonial Revival infatuation, Fowler created his most romantic visions of old Spain.

Here in Pasadena, he built three houses together, one inspired by the Basque region, another by the houses on the island of Majorca, and finally this replica of an Andalusian farmhouse, owned today by Shirley and Peter Porter. The house faces a trickling stone fountain on an expansive patio that these days doubles as a convenient circular drive and parking area for the current owners'

Jeeps and bicycles. Its plain whitewashed exterior is sheathed in vines that almost hide the rough wood doors. A verdant path leads to the main entrance in the rear of the house. The interior is informal and inviting, with polished wood beams and Spanish and Mexican wood furniture, as well as some American country pieces.

The exterior *corredores*, both upstairs and down, are used for year-round recreation and dining. A staircase graced with potted geraniums leads down to an ivy-covered wishing well, beyond which are a garden, pool, and cabaña. Were it not for the grand arches of the Colorado Street bridge, which can be seen from certain places in the gardens, it would be easy to forget that this farmhouse sits just blocks from busy city streets.

FAR LEFT: Geranium plants accentuate a tiled outdoor staircase that ascends from a courtyard to the second-story veranda, where the family gathers for games of pool. LEFT: African baskets and a dramatic cascading chrysanthemum are grouped on a Mexican table in the entry hall. The Welsh pine bench holds Indian blankets. ABOVE: The stone fountain in the center of the front patio harks back to simpler times. ABOVE RIGHT: Guests announce themselves by ringing a weathered bell before passing through heavily studded Spanish gates.

LEFT: The Porters' early-nineteenth-century French harvesting table and American Windsor chairs suit the country dining room. The corner fireplace mantel holds an Eskimo carving, while a fruit-filled lava bowl from Fiji creates a center-piece for the table. ABOVE RIGHT: The dark wood and massive proportions of the furniture complement the farmhouse's sturdy lines. Along one wall, an imposing wood carving hangs above a table crafted in Mexico and two Spanish chairs. A pair of Mission-style couches create a comfortable conversation area around a coffee table the owners made from an old Mexican door. Above the fireplace rests an Italian mosaic plaque. RIGHT: A French tapestry of old Seville casually draped across the wall carries out the Spanish theme in the master bedroom.

MILLIKAN HOUSE

LEFT: The focal point of this house, designed by architect Wallace Neff, is its informal central courtyard, both colorful and serene. A trickling fountain and vividly colored flora contribute to its warmth. Bright pink and white cyclamens growing in clay pots are neatly lined along what is actually the front of the house. Rather than feature a single formal front entrance, three sets of paired glass doors open onto the main hallway, a plan that both contributes to the house's sense of ease and opens it to the outdoors. ABOVE RIGHT: Visitors enter the courtyard through a low arched wall, where the owners have installed new wrought-iron gates and lighting fixtures. The woodwork and the shade of medium-blue paint on the doors are original to the house. TOP RIGHT: At the edge of the property, a wall designed in a graphic curve outlines a view of the San Gabriel Valley.

The hills of Flintridge can be both forbiddingly remote and rugged for city dwellers, but they command a breathtaking view of the San Gabriel Valley. This is the magnificent setting for the inviting Mexican-style aerie known as the Clark B. Millikan house (1931). The son of Nobel Prize–winning physicist Robert Millikan, Clark Millikan was a well-known member of the community.

L.A.'s celebrated Spanish Colonial Revivalist Wallace Neff was commissioned to build the house for Millikan and his wife, Helen. Turning to Mexico for inspiration, Neff designed a sprawling white-walled, tile-roofed *casa* with an enclosed central patio as the focal point.

The Millikan House is Neff's most authentic evocation of Mexican architecture and was one of his favorites. Visitors must cross the enclosed central patio to enter the house's main hallway through one of three pairs of French doors. The hall overlooks the massively beamed living room, one half-story below. On the same level are the dining room, breakfast area, and kitchen. Several years ago, the present owners, Edward and Gloria Renwick, set out to restore and enlarge the fountain, where lavender-blue water lilies now grow. The entire patio comes alive year round with brightly colored flowers planted in red tile pots.

LEFT: A patio off the living room at the back of the house is an ideal setting for informal alfresco dining and entertaining. The fanciful iron chandelier was part of the house's original design. Beyond the arched walls, just off to the side of the house, are steps leading to a formal rose garden. The grounds are luxuriously landscaped with citrus trees and a specimen cactus garden. BELOW: The living room is dominated by a fireplace adorned with a decorative shield believed to have been purchased by the Millikans. Neff designed the house so that when the tall double doors are opened, air circulates freely, eliminating the need for air-conditioning in the summer. Current owners Edward and Gloria Renwick have displayed their collection of nineteenth-century Chinese porcelain and jade throughout the house. Hanging beside the fireplace are nineteenth-century Chinese storefront panels.

ABOVE: A staircase paved with colorful tiles leads from the hallway to the living room below. LEFT: A late-eighteenth-century American credenza is poised in the hallway. A pair of Mexican tin sconces, installed when the house was first built, hang on either side.

MILLER/ MOUCK HOUSE

LEFT: At the turn of the century, the Fred Harvey Hotels, a chain of twenty-five small inns with restaurants and gift shops, sprouted up from Chicago to Southern California along the Santa Fe Railroad route. The hotels made an impact on tourists and southwestern culture and inspired the 1946 MGM film *The Harvey Girls*, starring Judy Garland and Angela Lansbury. For homeowners J. Evan Miller and Richard Mouck, souvenirs from the Harvey gift shops, which were open for business through the 1950s, have become a fascination. On the living-room mantel they display tourist items, including miniature Navajo rugs, tiny terracotta models of California's Franciscan missions, Indian basketry, and bronze miniature animals. The numerous bells, signed by artisan Mary Forbes, were sold in mission gift shops in the twenties. The Craftsman-style clocks were featured in early Sears Roebuck catalogs.

The stone fireplace is made of California jade and quartz, with Malibu Potteries tiles on the hearth. ABOVE: In keeping with the mission spirit of old California, the owners designed and constructed a bell tower atop their home. TOP RIGHT: On the dining-room wall is a Two Grey Hills Navajo rug. The deer-antler chandelier was crafted in an artist's studio in Pasadena's Arroyo Culture colony.

Fifty-seven steps lead up to the front door of J. Evan Miller and Richard Mouck's hillside home. The house is a personal statement that reflects the owners' passionate interest in the Southwest and early Californiana. Miller and Mouck transformed an ordinary bungalow at the top of Goat Hill in the Eagle Rock district into their own form of Mission Revival expressionism.

Inspired by turn-of-the-century postcards depicting mission grounds, the landmark Mission Inn in Riverside, and their travels to the sites of the missions, the men began turning the house into a shrine of sorts in 1978. A garden, filled with lantana and citrus trees, is planted in a cruciform pattern with a central fountain. The surrounding beds are overflowing with oleander, lantana, aloe, rosemary, yucca, and citrus, evoking images of arid mission grounds and, incidentally, successfully functioning as a drought-resistant garden. Pathways lead to a whimsical campanile, which the owners affixed to an upstairs balcony.

The bell motif is repeated hundreds of times throughout the gardens and inside the house, recalling the turn of the century, when bell collecting was a popular way to bring the mission feeling home.

Bells are only one of the owners' extraordinary collections, assembled in baroque excess. Miniature missions, Indian rugs, baskets, rosaries, and even Hollywood memorabilia fill the house.

OPPOSITE PAGE: Ten steps lead from the courtyard patio to the base of the bell tower. Each colorful riser is decorated with a different pattern of 1920s tile manufactured by American Encaustic Tiling Co., a firm in Vernon, near downtown Los Angeles. At the top is a wrought-iron candelabrum designed by Miller and Mouck, and at the bottom is an altar accessory. LEFT, MIDDLE: This intricately carved altarpiece once stood in the now remodeled Santa Theresa Church in Sierra Madre. Today, Miller and Mouck feature it prominently in their living room, where it rests on a Bible stand imported from Spain. More than 200 rosaries, dozens of crosses, and a mission-period holy-water dispenser complete the ecclesiastical display. All of the house's religious pieces have been collected at antique shops, swap meets, and estate sales, and on trips throughout the world. LEFT, TOP: Archangel Michael and a mission bell greet visitors as they pass through a simple wooden gate that leads to a lush plant-filled entrance tunnel. At night the passageway and steps are illuminated by dozens of candles. LEFT, BOTTOM: In the courtyard patio adjoining the bedroom, a potted garden surrounds the spa as flowering snail vines drape over the garden walls. The fountain is covered with a mix of American Encaustic and French tiles. Above it is a niche holding another mission bell. The ironwork is from a Mexican hacienda.

FAR LEFT: For the home-owners, the golden age of Hollywood was as integral to the history of California as the missions, and movieland memorabilia show up in several rooms. On the kitchen wall, ceramic masks of film legends set the nostalgic mood. The entrance to the breakfast room is marked with a gate of Art Deco grillwork. The Art Deco chandelier once lit a Mary See's Candy Shop. ABOVE LEFT: The 1938 General Electric refrigerator, with its circular refrigeration unit on top, and the 1937 Magic Chef stove are still working in the kitchen. ABOVE: Miller and Mouck have their own Hollywood movie palace, which seats twenty. Decorated as it might have been in the thirties, the little auditorium has an antique tin ceiling complete with bullet holes. An asbestos theater curtain came from the Belmont Theater in downtown L.A. The vintage tassels and lanterns once hung in movie studios and cinemas. LEFT: The bedroom is a virtual sheik's den inspired by the overstatements of twenties film-set decorators. Here, in Moorish profusion, the dresser is loaded with brass trinkets. On the bed are favorite souvenir pillows from the twenties.

KEATING CABIN

FAR LEFT: The living room of this charming cabin, with its split-log walls, was the original owner's personal interpretation of rustic living in 1924, when the house was completed. Little has changed three quarters of a century later. The dining-room table, animal heads, and lighting fixtures, including the hand-cut silhouette chandelier, are still intact. The current owners, Kathy and Larry Keating, have appropriately added a tablescape of Adirondack tramp-art log-cabin boxes and pink sweet peas arranged in milk bottles. ABOVE: Situated atop a hill overlooking a lush canyon filled with avant-garde architecture, this classic log cabin looks the same as it did when the Uplifters Club was in full swing.

T he canyons surrounding Los Angeles are considered among the city's choicest environs. Carved into the Santa Monica Mountains, the aptly named Rustic Canyon was once the retreat of the city's most powerful politicians and businessmen. The Uplifters Club, founded in 1913, was a raucous offshoot of downtown's exclusive Los Angeles Athletic Club. Among the members were L. Frank Baum, the author of *The Wizard of Oz*, and filmmaker Hal Roach, who created the "Our Gang" comedies.

In 1920, the Uplifters Clubhouse was built on 80 acres of lush real estate in the heart of the Canyon. But it's the enclave of log cabins, most of them designed by Alfred and Arthur Heineman, in the surrounding foothills that holds the most charm.

In a curious twist of Hollywood fantasy, some of the cabins—including this one—were lifted from the Lake Ar-

rowhead stage set for the 1920s film *The Courtship of Miles Standish*. Banker Marco Hellman, an original member of the Uplifters Club, lived in the faux log cabin pictured. This wood frame house with half-logs applied to both the interior and the exterior is a study in warmth and whimsy. Alfred Heineman designed an interior for the Hollywood façade and created the rustic furniture—such as barrel couches, chairs, and tables, and an imposing grandfather clock—that remains intact today. The lighting fixtures show silhouettes of Hellman and his children frolicking outdoors.

Present owners Larry and Kathy Keating have added their own homespun touches, including a collection of log cabin boxes, twig furniture, and a few well-placed quilts. Mrs. Keating, a landscape designer, maintains the grounds in a tangled display of California color. In the springtime, roses climb to the roof of the house and wildflowers mix with bulbs, cymbidium orchids, herbs, and vegetables.

LEFT: Close inspection of an iron sconce, designed for the house, reveals a whimsical bat whose eyes are wired to flash. ABOVE: Eucalyptus trunks support a balcony used as a reading corner and create a cozy built-in seating area underneath. The coffee table, with its barrel base, is original to the house. Kathy Keating's quilts decorate the walls and pillows.

ABOVE: The Keatings have steadfastly maintained the Uplifters' romantic spirit in their urban log cabin, which once served as the summer home of former California governor and U.S. Supreme Court Chief Justice Earl Warren and his family. Like all the cabin's owners, the Keatings have inherited many of its unique furnishings, including the barrel couch seen here. They have added compatible pieces of their own, including twig furniture from Appalachia and Northern California, basketry, antique clothing, and Larry's teacup collection, housed in a glass cabinet. A steerhorn design defines the imposing weather-worn stone fireplace with its hand-forged iron grates. LEFT: In the living room, a Dutch doll's chair hangs above a family portrait.

SIMON HOUSE

FAR LEFT: The plain lines of crude Mexican furniture create a simple setting in Roger Simon's master bedroom. The wooden bed was newly made to mix with the old chairs and small chest. An austere copper lamp casts a glow on ocher and gold walls, while natural light passes through muslin curtains. Simon purchased the striped cover on the bed while trekking through Nepal. **LEFT:** Simon's house scales a hillside, and at the lowest level is a black-bottomed swimming pool. Two of Simon's balconies overlook the pool and the lush canyon below. The smaller balcony, supported with classical columns, adjoins the dining room. The larger porch, with its picnic table and benches, can accommodate a crowd for outdoor dining. **ABOVE RIGHT:** For a sense of additional space and privacy, Simon added a traditional Mexican wall to the front of his property. The nineteenth-century Mexican doors are made of mesquite wood.

Secluded in the Hollywood Hills and surrounded by eucalyptus groves, this typically Spanish L.A. house, built in 1929, recently has been recast as a warm, inviting, rustic Mexican *casa*. When the owner, screenwriter and novelist Roger Simon, bought the house in 1988, it had been completely modernized save for its characteristic red tile roof. Based on his belief that "Southern California *is* Mexico—there's a karma about it," Simon first set out to restore the house's Spanish lines. He added tiled porches for dining and a high protective wall punctuated with decorative tiles, creating a private, plant-filled front courtyard.

The dramatic use of color, both inside and out, was based on Simon's love of the vibrant architecture of Mexico's Luis Barragan as well as on his memories of traveling through provincial Mexican villages around Guanajuato and San Miguel de Allende. To work up a suitable palette of ochers, blues, reds, lavenders, and greens, Simon enlisted the help of decorative arts historian Julia Winston and artist Brent Spears.

Exterior and interior walls are muted and seem to have been weathering for a century. Sofas and chairs are slipcovered in natural and dyed linens. All the wood furniture in the house is rough-hewn oak and pine, imported from Mexico. Lively striped serapes, draped across chairs and hung as curtains, add splashes of strong color, along with Mexican ceramics and folk art.

LEFT: Hand-painted wainscoting creates a geometric pattern around the dining room. The old rush-and-wood chairs are Mexican, as is the ceramic bowl. Hanging on the wall in the living room is a decorative panel from a carousel depicting the life of Benito Juárez, who grew from shepherd boy to heroic president of Mexico.

LEFT: "Because I work in theater, I like theatricality, and I see my house as something of a set," says Simon, explaining why he turned his home into a vivid rendition of the simple Mexican *casas* he's so fond of. A turquoise wall, punctuated with a crimson door, and an ocher linen slipcovered sofa add touches of old-world color. On the blue trunk from the Philippines stands a Guatemalan skeleton figure. Although Simon likes to live in an environment of uncomplicated south-of-the-border design, his office in the loft above the living room is fully equipped with a computer and other modern office machines.

ABOVE: Simon's kitchen was conceived with the orange and yellow colors of a José Cuervo tequila advertisement in mind. The brightly painted cabinet fits perfectly into the scheme. Simon repainted the chairs turquoise.
RIGHT: Fresh air breezes into the bathroom and over the nineteenth-century wood-and-copper tub. **TOP RIGHT:** A western-style chair is set before shelves lined with pre-Columbian ceramic art in the reading room.

HALL/RIVA HOUSE

FAR LEFT: For Stella Hall and Michael Riva, a western-style chair upholstered in cowhide and a rustic forged iron-and-wood table make an inviting place to kick back in the master bedroom. Sun filters through glass doors that lead to a small deck overlooking the garden, playhouse, and spa. ABOVE: A bronco-buster on his bucking mount is the knocker on the bottle-green front door of this Spanish-style house.

The Wild West maintains a powerful grip on inhabitants of Los Angeles, even though the closest most Angelenos have come to it is the Ford Broncos parked in their driveways. California's cowboy past exists primarily in the imagination or in vague memories of Hollywood westerns. With few tangible reminders of the region's rough-and-tumble days, people here are drawn to movie symbolism. Early-twentieth-century cowboy kitsch and true rustic furniture of the Spanish Colonial era are now prized collectibles that lend homes an air of history and belonging.

Hollywood production designer Michael Riva and his wife, actress Stella Hall, found that they didn't need to live on a cattle ranch to express their love of the West. They've furnished their 1920s Spanish Colonial Revival house with all manner of Western furniture.

Among their prized possessions are old California desert landscape paintings, a contemporary folk-art bed, and a cowboy-style sofa and chairs from the now collectible Monterey line of home furnishings, manufactured and sold in the thirties and forties by the Los Angeles retailer Barker Brothers. For a finishing touch, Hall and Riva enlisted Hollywood scenic painters to decorate some of their walls and cabinetry with cowboys and lassos.

Hall's and Riva's affection for the West is also evident outdoors in a playful mix of potted cacti and cowboy kitsch—even their Jacuzzi gets western-ized. They stationed a log-cabin playhouse in the garden for their son, John Michael. And on the hottest days, he can run through a sprinkler, a miniature wrangler spouting water.

LEFT: The living room, viewed through an arched doorway, is a homey space packed with books and family mementos. A collection of ranch-house furniture includes the sofa, lounge chair, end tables, and coffee table. A pair of table lamps feature parchment shades superimposed with photographic transparencies of the Old West. **ABOVE:** In the dining room, Mexican children's chairs and a sombrero from Olvera Street are hung from the rafters for a whimsical touch. A miniature tobacco barn sits on the buffet beneath a Jeff Joyce landscape painting.

ABOVE: The landscape above the fireplace was originally painted for a western movie set. Dispersed throughout the living room are such disparate decorative touches as family photographs in Victorian sterling frames, Italian Murano glass, old Mexican serapes, and Skookum Indian dolls. **BELOW:** Even the kitchen, with all its modern conveniences, harks back to cowboy days. Hanging overhead are the appropriate strings of lights, interspersed with cactus and chili peppers, while collections of salt and pepper shakers, cookie jars, and mugs carry out the theme. The bowls and serving platters are early Fiesta and Bauer pottery.

ABOVE: In the master bedroom, the head-board, designed by L. D. Burke, is embellished with spurs and horse-shoes that spell out the message "Sweet Dreams." In contrast to this rusticity is a fluffy cloud of white linens and, above the bed, a trio of Italian cherubs. LEFT: On top of the painted chest of draw-ers, which is stamped with the Monterey brand, is a collection of Old California bric-a-brac culled from flea markets and local galleries.

LEFT: A wrangler spinning his lasso is actually a concrete sprinkler nurturing the lawn. **BELOW:** John Michael Riva gets his own version of cowboy style in one corner of the back forty. The playhouse log cabin was ordered from the Sears catalog, and a stick horse is propped over his bunk. A small birdhouse hangs under the eaves.

ABOVE: Hall and Riva's backyard space doubles as a place for work and play. A detached room serves as both guesthouse and office, and children can cavort on the lawn when they're not in the playhouse. A formal, semicircular sculpted hedge outlines a whimsical space for entertaining. A cigar-store Indian stands guard at one end of a redwood-and-wrought-iron pergola, where an iron horseshoe brand dangles overhead. Near the brick barbecue pit, a ceramic Mexican *ranchero* takes a siesta, shaded by his sombrero. The silver glass ball resting in a cement birdbath reflects the noonday sun.

What color *is* Los Angeles? Every Angeleno views the city differently.

"I see green and beige —palm trees and stucco. It's Stucco City."

"There's a kaleidoscope of soda-fountain colors, especially on the houses."

Colorations

"On certain stretches, like on Santa Monica Boulevard in West Hollywood, all you see are neon colors."

"Green lawns, blue pools. There are lots of cool colors."

LEFT: When it was designed in the thirties by architects William Wurdeman and William O. Becket, the Pan Pacific Auditorium was an exuberant celebration of color and Streamline Moderne design. Its glaring green façade, above which are stacks of four elliptical pylons sprouting flagpoles, turned the building into a traffic stopper in the Fairfax district. The auditorium was destroyed by fire in 1989. ABOVE RIGHT: In the spring, the California poppy, the state flower, adds brilliant orange fire to West Coast hillsides and urban street scenes. In Los Angeles, poppies crop up in unexpected places—at the bases of parking meters or, as here, in an otherwise dull, dry field. RIGHT: In a small bathroom in the exquisite Adamson House (see page 115), solid sea-blue tiles and multicolored accent pieces from Malibu Potteries cover every inch of the room. A child's book inspired designer Donald Prouty to create the ship-motif tiles.

The fact is, Los Angeles is all those colors—pastel, neon, grass green, swimming-pool blue—all set against an equally variegated palette of storefronts, restaurants, cars, billboards, murals, graffiti, and vegetation. Adding to it all are the city's extremely colorful people, who are likely to wear fluorescent athletic clothes in one end of the city and, in a close-knit K'anjobal Indian community on another side of town, to dress in the richly colored weavings of Guatemala.

The land itself displays the most intense palette: gray and silver native chaparral blends into the dry brown hillsides like army camouflage. Fiery yellow mustard plants erupt next to pink flowering ice plants on the mountains along the coastline. Golden-orange California poppies, the state's official flower, blanket inland fields.

And without fail, houses both grand and diminutive are sheathed in vivid flora.

Fuchsia bougainvillea, orange birds of paradise, purple irises, and tropical green palms abound. Manicured carpets of lawn are punctuated with lemon, orange, and avocado trees. The locals are so proud of their rose gardens that they hold a spectacle each year, Pasadena's Tournament of Roses Parade on New Year's Day, to pay tribute to

BELOW: In Los Angeles's Chinatown, the strong reds, yellows, and blues of the Far East have been part of the downtown street scene since the area first developed, in the 1870s. BELOW LEFT: When the huge Richfield Oil Company Building was erected in 1928, it was the tallest building in the city and was crowned with one of the most powerful aviation beacons in the state. But it was equally dazzling for nighttime passersby, since its spectacular art deco–moderne lines were highlighted in neon. By day, its black tile walls glistened with gold trim. The building, designed by Morgan, Walls & Clements, was demolished in 1972 to make room for the paired modern towers in today's Atlantic Richfield Plaza.

the flower that grows so heartily here.

In the past, however, people have been rather opinionated when it comes to the pigment of their architecture. Perhaps that's because they are bombarded by so much color just walking out their front doors or driving down the street. They demolished, or let nature demolish, both the black-and-gold Richfield Building (constructed in 1928) and the celery-green Pan-Pacific Auditorium (built in 1935). Yet they continue to boast about the magentas, vermilions, aquas, and yellows that adorned the city during the 1984 Olympic Games.

Still, white has been the predominant choice since the Franciscans whitewashed their adobe mission walls. Drive down any Los Angeles residential block and the common denominator among the crazy mix of architectural styles is the white or off-white paint. The stained brown wood of early-Craftsman bungalows is commonly whited-out now too. The California modernists of the twenties, thirties, and forties—subscribing to strict International Style philosophy—used white with a vengeance.

When it comes to color, the subject of the brilliant southern California sun almost always arises. One school of thought maintains that a bright sun demands intense color. Pragmatists contend that as in other Mediterranean or tropical climes, a hot sun will bleach colors, so white is the purely logical choice. Still others take a more romantic approach and argue the appeal of white: when illuminated by the full force of the brilliant sunlight, white structures sparkle. In the late afternoon, when the sun bathes the city in a golden glow, it casts rosy shadows across the white houses dotting the cityscape. (So beloved are sunsets here, as the late architectural critic Reyner Banham observed in his book *Los Angeles: The Architecture of Four Ecologies*, that the city named one of its greatest boulevards after the daily phenomenon.) Architect

ABOVE: The temporary structures of the 1984 Summer Olympics, held in Los Angeles, created an "instant architecture" that transformed the existing streets and buildings of the city. Designed and conceived by Jon Jerde of the Jerde Partnership, Main Street in the Olympic Village was made of painted construction scaffolding, fabric, and plywood panels. The colors, created by Deborah Sussman and Paul Prejza of Sussman/Prejza & Co., were first called those of "mariachi federalism," but later, to avoid Mexican overtones, were designated "festive federalism."

BELOW: The vibrant hue of this hibiscus that flourishes in Los Angeles is part of what has been called the "quintessentially California" Olympic palette. According to Jon Jerde, lead architect of the group that worked on the Los Angeles Olympics, color was "the main thread that held the work of forty-three design firms together."

ABOVE and RIGHT: When the Pacific Design Center was unveiled in 1975, it was the talk of the town. Some called it a masterpiece; some called it a mistake. The work of architect Cesar Pelli, who was then working with Victor Gruen Associates, the huge blue glass structure dominated more than 500 feet on then-sleepy Melrose Avenue, in the center of the interior-design district. The overscale "Blue Whale," as it is still familiarly known, transformed the neighborhood into a bustling business center, and Melrose eventually blossomed into a trendy shopping street. Now joined by a green wing, and with a red one on its way, the Design Center is surrounded with gardens, plazas, and a fountain.

Cesar Pelli has written that when seen in the Los Angeles light, "white is a positive and strong color" against the blue sky. Nevertheless, Pelli's most famous local building is the "Blue Whale," the affectionate name for the Pacific Design Center (1975), a solid-blue glass mass now joined by an all-green glass addition. A third glass structure—this time in red—is now planned.

While the Victorians preferred a showy palette of deep reds, greens, and pinks, in more recent times it has taken the occasional rebel to integrate vivid paint colors onto the faces of houses. Charles and Ray Eames's Case Study House in Pacific Palisades (1949), incorporating black, white, and primary colors, looks like a three-dimensional Mondrian painting. Architect Lloyd Wright, son of Frank Lloyd

BELOW: Pasadena's Rose Bowl flea market is a popular spot for inspecting the vibrant decorative arts that have emanated from Los Angeles for decades. Pictured here is an array of collectible pottery, much of it crafted in the thirties and forties.

ABOVE: Integral to Frank Gehry's design for Loyola University Law School are the architect's bold blocks of orange, ocher, and green.

ABOVE: With the Pacific Ocean in the background to amplify the blue of its tiles, the peacock fountain on the east patio at Malibu's Adamson House (see page 115) is a masterpiece of custom tile work. The intricately patterned tiles were designed at the family-owned Malibu Potteries, using the *cuerda seca* technique, a Spanish and Moorish glazing process that results in brilliant colors outlined in black. In addition to the large peacock, tiny birds are hidden among the flowers in the background.

Wright, favored strong colors in his Johnson House (now the residence of film director David Lynch) in Hollywood (1963), using assertive violet and green paint both inside and out. Still, most of Lloyd Wright's clients shied away from bold color statements and preferred safer earth tones, according to his son, architect Eric Lloyd Wright.

Starting in the seventies, color gradually began gaining acceptance by a new generation of architects, including Charles Moore, who integrated twenty-eight colors inside and out at the Burns House in Pacific Palisades (1974). Other brilliantly colored buildings are Frank Gehry's green, ocher, and orange Loyola Law School (1984), the Jerde Partnership's Westside Pavilion (1985), with its magenta, aqua, yellow, and scarlet accents, and architectural designer Josh Schweitzer's Border Grill restaurant (1990) in Santa Monica, with its explosively colorful primitive murals. Many young architects and interior designers acknowledge the influence of strong color statements by Mexican architects Luis Barragan and Ricardo Legorreta. They are recognizing that the city's proximity and historical ties to Mexico as well as its large Hispanic population are integral to L.A.'s identity.

For most of the century, the strongest use of color has come from the Hispanic and Asian cultures. Downtown's Chinatown is embellished in lacquer red and yellow and must have inspired American architects Meyer and Holler to construct the riotous colossus known as the Grauman's Chinese Theatre in Hollywood

BAUER
1941 California Pottery Catalog Reprint

McBean and Co. (later known as Franciscan), and J. A. Bauer. Throughout the thirties and forties, Bauer's California Colored line of tableware, flowerpots, and urns was glazed in hot Mexican colors such as orange, yellow, and cobalt blue. It predated the more commonly known Fiesta tableware manufactured in West Virginia by the Homer Laughlin China Company. Though Bauer closed shop in the early sixties, the resurgence of interest in its products among collectors is apparent at any Sunday morning flea market in Southern California.

The creative community continues to thrive on the colors of the city, from the landscapes of David Hockney and the pop statements of Ed Ruscha and Billy Al Bengston to the furniture and ceramics of Peter Shire, some of which have been produced by the Italian design group Memphis.

For many of the people who live here, creating an environment filled with vibrant objects, furniture, and art, and designing with color, have become ways to express individuality and to be adventurous. They also declare an acceptance of the city's present—a merging of inventive artists working within a multicultural tableau—and of its past.

(1927). And a new multicolored Korean Buddhist temple stands out among bland gas stations and supermarkets near downtown Los Angeles.

The Spanish Colonial Revival movement of the twenties spawned the use of pastel façades as well as the ubiquitous beige stucco, and also the widespread use of terra-cotta roofs and colorful, decorative tiles both indoors and out. In 1926, May K. Rindge and her husband Frederick Hastings Rindge, the last owners of the Spanish land grant that is identified today as Malibu, founded the Malibu Potteries to meet the demand for multicolored ceramic tiles (see page 115). They were a vivid contrast to the muted earth tones used by Pasadena's Ernest Batchelder during the Arts and Crafts era.

The Malibu tiles featured Moorish, Mayan, and art deco designs as well as stylized plant motifs. They appeared on doorways, pediments, fireplace mantels, garden fountains, stair treads and risers, tabletops, and urns in homes from Beverly Hills to Santa Ana. Public buildings such as Los Angeles City Hall, the Los Angeles Public Library, and the Mayan Theater also were encrusted with tiles made by Malibu Potteries.

Other commercial pottery companies flourished in Los Angeles, including Catalina, Pacific, Meyers, Metlox, Gladding

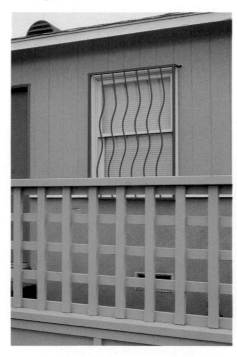

ADAMSON HOUSE

Picture a beach that goes on for miles along the coast of Santa Monica Bay, with a magnificent view of Catalina Island to the south, where the pounding waves attract surfers from the world over and movie stars have built their own colony to escape the madding crowd—this is Malibu Beach. Now imagine the most desirable location on that beach—that is the site of Adamson House, a Spanish-Moorish Colonial Revival home built in 1929.

Designed by architect Stiles O. Clements and decorated by John B. Holtzclaw and the artisans of the renowned Malibu Potteries, the house is a feast for the eyes—that is, for those eyes that love ornamentation. Thousands of colorful Malibu Potteries tiles are lavishly splashed throughout the gardens, patios, and interior, each room having its own unique theme, motifs, and colors.

Fanciful wrought iron accents windows, railings, and balconies, while hand-painted murals create a delicate counterpart to the dramatic and varied tiles.

Malibu Potteries was founded in 1926 to meet the needs of architects and designers who were hungry for vivid tile work that would add touches of authentic pattern and color to their projects, whether of Spanish Colonial, Mediterranean, Islamic, or Moorish inspiration. Entrepreneur May K. Rindge established the factory on the beach just east of Malibu pier with Rufus B. Keeler, one of the most talented ceramists in the country, as the creative force. His secret formula resulted in vibrant hues with extraordinary clarity.

Mrs. Rindge's daughter, Rhoda, and her husband, Merritt Adamson, built this grand house as a beach cottage for their family. The original furnishings, still on display in the home today, reflect the casual elegance of the period. Originally part of one of California's most beautiful land grants, Rancho Topanga, Malibu y Sequit, the Adamson House is now protected as part of Malibu Lagoon Park. It is listed on the National Register of Historic Places and is also recorded as a California Historical Landmark.

RIGHT: The main entrance to the house is a solid-teak door with Bavarian bottle-glass windows. The original colors painted on the molded concrete above the door have been gently faded by the sun. Along the sides runs a pattern of brilliantly colored Saracen-style tiles.

LEFT: Though the Pacific Ocean is but a short walk away, the Adamsons built a grand saltwater pool, duly bordered in tiles, and an adjacent poolhouse. In the distance is Malibu Pier. **ABOVE:** Beautiful wrought-iron doors lead to the house's interior loggia. The grapevine design was once brilliantly hand-painted. Today, though the doors are still glorious, only hints of the old colors appear. Many of the ceilings, both inside and out, were painted by two Danish artists, Ejnar Hansen and Peter Nielsen, who were part of decorator John B. Holtzclaw's design team. As the family believed in punctuality, the bell between doors was one of many around the house. Even the strawberry pot was manufactured at the family's factory. **RIGHT:** The only stairway at this seashore mansion features a skylight that casts a gentle glow on the ocher walls. The decorative baseboard skirting in bright blue, orange, and black-patterned tiles was designed to match the stair risers. The stairs lead to family bedrooms, a second kitchen, and nurse's quarters.

LEFT: The first thing visitors see when they enter this grand abode is an ornate wrought-iron table surfaced with 45 tiles, which was designed by Inez Johnson von Hake, a designer and illustrator at Malibu Potteries. A fanciful grille decorates an interior window that looks through to the loggia and, beyond, toward the ocean. The pot and large jar are Italian faience, collected on family trips to Europe. ABOVE: In the kitchen is one of two sinks surrounded by vivid ceramic tiles. BELOW: A Moorish-style picture window affords a commanding view of the Pacific from the main dining room. The cast plaster ceiling was painted to look like wood by Hansen and Nielsen, who also worked on the historic Biltmore Hotel on downtown Los Angeles's Pershing Square. The iron chandelier was made locally by B. B. Bell and Sons. The turquoise jardiniere on the hearth came from the family's factories. RIGHT: This charming tiled room adjacent to the kitchen was the butler's pantry and also served as a sunny dining room for the servants. Intense shades of marine blue and persimmon, with dramatic black accents, are continued throughout the kitchen. The rectangular tile mural depicting a classical urn and flowers was designed by William Handley, a draftsman, artist, and designer at the Malibu Potteries. The walls are skirted in vibrant Saracen-style tiles, and the floors feature alternating patterns. The table and heavy Spanish-style leather chairs, like all the furniture pictured, are original to the home.

CAPLIS HOUSE

FAR LEFT: Echoing the dynamic lines of the living room of Joan Caplis's house is a dramatic Moderne couch. Fashioned in the thirties, the sofa is upholstered with a striking geometric pattern in shades of mauve, aqua, and gold, based on a design by architect Walter Gropius, founder of the Bauhaus school. Complementing the sofa's curves is a chunky side chair in hot-pink polished cotton. The painting on the mantel is by Gerrit W. van Sinclair, a WPA artist of the thirties. The green vase alongside it is a piece of Weller pottery. LEFT, MIDDLE: The small house, with its arresting front door, sits on a quiet street on a hilltop near the ocean. LEFT, TOP: In the den, designer Lori Erenberg has created the feeling of an old Hawaiian lanai by using early-forties bamboo furniture and the distinctive tropical prints of the period.

There's nothing tame about the fuchsia front door and the canary yellow jardiniere that give this Streamline Moderne beach bungalow (1939) its curb appeal. Joan Caplis lives among colors that she frankly refers to as "thirties French boudoir—a feminine palette of pinks, aquas, and yellows." The hits of color come primarily from upholstery, painted walls, and geometrically patterned linoleum. The ebullient shades are intensified by quiet background colors, so that even a small vase of amaryllis flowers immediately catches the eye.

Caplis worked in collaboration with her childhood friend, Lori Erenberg, a colorist and interior designer, who has a special affinity for early-modern L.A. houses. They stalked vintage furniture stores for the curvaceous furniture that complements the curves of the original fireplace.

CAPLIS HOUSE

FAR LEFT: Echoing the dynamic lines of the living room of Joan Caplis's house is a dramatic Moderne couch. Fashioned in the thirties, the sofa is upholstered with a striking geometric pattern in shades of mauve, aqua, and gold, based on a design by architect Walter Gropius, founder of the Bauhaus school. Complementing the sofa's curves is a chunky side chair in hot-pink polished cotton. The painting on the mantel is by Gerrit W. van Sinclair, a WPA artist of the thirties. The green vase alongside it is a piece of Weller pottery. **LEFT, MIDDLE:** The small house, with its arresting front door, sits on a quiet street on a hilltop near the ocean. **LEFT, TOP:** In the den, designer Lori Erenberg has created the feeling of an old Hawaiian lanai by using early-forties bamboo furniture and the distinctive tropical prints of the period.

There's nothing tame about the fuchsia front door and the canary yellow jardiniere that give this Streamline Moderne beach bungalow (1939) its curb appeal. Joan Caplis lives among colors that she frankly refers to as "thirties French boudoir—a feminine palette of pinks, aquas, and yellows." The hits of color come primarily from upholstery, painted walls, and geometrically patterned linoleum. The ebullient shades are intensified by quiet background colors, so that even a small vase of amaryllis flowers immediately catches the eye.

Caplis worked in collaboration with her childhood friend, Lori Erenberg, a colorist and interior designer, who has a special affinity for early-modern L.A. houses. They stalked vintage furniture stores for the curvaceous furniture that complements the curves of the original fireplace.

CORNELL/ BENNETT HOUSE

FAR LEFT: The walled garden at the back of Kathleen Cornell and Chuck Bennett's Venice home is used as a year-round retreat, both day and night. It functions as an extension of the house and as an out-door room for dining and entertaining. A vintage Pacific Pottery vase filled with sun-flowers sits on one of four symmetrically placed cement-block benches. In the center of the space is a mirror-topped wrought-iron garden table and chairs. ABOVE: A green frame, affectionately called the "emerald gate" by Cornell and Bennett, outlines an office entrance. The leap-ing-trout night-light is a reference to Bennett's favorite hobby.

White walls wouldn't do for Kathleen Cornell and Chuck Bennett's trans-formed forties duplex. Perhaps because Cornell, a pho-tographer's agent, and Bennett, an advertising art director, are such colorful types, they chose to surround themselves with intense hues. A combination of brilliant purple, Chinese yellow, emerald, jade, and teal might be too much for the average eye, but this couple believes the vibrant colors allow them to create "warmth without clutter." Says Cornell, "We're not into window coverings or gewgaws."

Color was also an instant and inexpensive way to de-fine spaces and add "architectural character" where none existed. "The house was nondescript—it didn't enclose us," recalls Cornell. "Because we have the luxury of being outdoors morning, noon, and night, we like the feeling of

retreating inside to our nest."

In the process of converting from a two-unit duplex house to a single-family dwelling, the couple eliminated doors and enlarged passageways between rooms to give a sense of spatial flow. A "middle room," formerly a bedroom, is similar in concept to a foyer except that it's in the center of the house and exists purely to add a sense of lavish space in an otherwise tiny environment. Also contributing to the spaciousness are a few well-chosen furnishings, from flea-market finds to contemporary Italian art furniture.

A symmetrical arrangement of palm trees and concrete sofas turns the home's backyard into a "post-nuclear classical Italian garden," says Venice landscape artist Jay Griffith, who carved the monolithic benches from the solid concrete that previously paved the area.

The owners, in turn, see their garden as a comfortable place to be at leisure. When entertaining, they roll out a Persian carpet and dine on an old garden table fitted with a mirrored surface that reflects the Mexican yuccas and agaves that proliferate in the garden. Color emanates from the dominant purple back wall and the matching flowering ice plant.

RIGHT: The colors of the dining room are rather sedate compared to the rest of the house. It is painted a soft pearl gray and is bathed in sunlight throughout most of the day. Massimo Iosa-Ghini designed the "Notorious" armchairs. The far wall is dominated by a monoprint by Edgar Peais, a San Francisco artist.

FAR LEFT: The owners used explosive colors to give each room its distinct character. Past the house's Chinese-yellow "middle room," the deep-purple walls of the salon set off a pair of leopard-print upholstered couches. The couches are the only furniture in the room, save for a solid-marble table designed by Giusti and DiRosa. The silver tea set belonged to Cornell's grandmother, and the silver vase holding a spray of cerise-colored carnations was found in a flea market. **LEFT:** The color scheme in the yellow middle room includes a "tufted" teal-green door. The standing brass lamp, one of a pair, is a swap-meet find. **ABOVE:** Bennett keeps his electric guitar on view in the living room so that he can admire it at all times. Outside, seen through a bank of windows, is a salvaged iron urn that lends a classical note.

LaVASSER/ WALTERS HOUSE

A resplendent collection of Los Angeles–made J. A. Bauer pottery creates a dazzling display of color in this contemporary house. The vividly glazed pottery, manufactured from 1929 through the 1950s, was one of the city's proudest exports. The collection amassed here by Gary LaVasser and Dan Walters illustrates the wide range of designs produced by the company, from teapots to flowerpots and all manner of accessories for the table.

It is the collection of rare Bauer oil jars made in the early thirties that best depicts the rainbow of glazes that were fired in the Bauer kilns, northeast of downtown Los Angeles. LaVasser and Walters are also drawn to the fluid hand-thrown art pottery designed by Matt Carlton, which was produced by the company as a sideline to its more commercial designs. Many of Carlton's finest pieces predate

the popular colored tableware, having been produced as early as the teens. Most of Carlton's designs are classically inspired vases and flower bowls in a soft green glaze, and most of them are unsigned.

Also on shelves in the homeowners' cabinets are hundreds of pieces of other collectible tableware, produced in Los Angeles by the Gladding McBean and Franciscan pottery companies. LaVasser and Walters scour the country in search of additions to their vast collection, which celebrates the colorful past of Los Angeles.

BELOW: Displayed on the sideboard is a complete set of a long-necked water bottle and glasses in a wrought-iron holder, once used for outdoor entertaining. The set survived an earthquake and remains one of the owners' most prized finds. On the wall is an oil painting, *Ingres on Art*, from a series by LaVasser. Variegated Dutch tulips overflowing from Bauer vases complete the still life.

BELOW: Though LaVasser and Walters are partial to Bauer, they also collect other pottery from the same period that was produced in Los Angeles. Among the more unusual items is this Santa Anita dinnerware featuring the city flower of Los Angeles. The "Bird of Paradise" pattern was manufactured in the late forties. Today, it sets an inviting table **for alfresco dining on the deck adjoining the kitchen. BELOW LEFT: Sought-after Bauer oil jars, collected in nearly a dozen shades, form a rainbow in front of a stark black tile fireplace. The owners are such fans of the distinctive oil jars that they also commissioned fiberglass copies, like the yellow one holding the flowers in the foreground. BELOW: Cupboards are bursting with colorful pieces of ringed Bauer pottery. The counter is filled with Matt Carlton's artful designs. The large and small jade-green vases on the table are Carlton's Rebecca jars.**

LEFT: Mass-produced and handmade pots and vases are perched at every level in and around the dining room, creating a vivid display. The owners juxtapose the rounded pottery with the industrial, angular design of Marcel Breuer's Wassily chair and furniture sold in the twenties by Los Angeles's Barker Brothers.

ROWE HOUSE

FAR LEFT: Divergent patterns of vibrant color merge on the walls, bed, and windows of this small master bedroom in Van-Martin Rowe's bungalow. The classic Mexican blanket on the bed sharply contrasts with the dynamic mixed-media collage by Cammie Warner that hangs on the mushroom-and-eggplant walls. Refracting the afternoon light and adding more hues to the scene is a 1920s stained-glass window. ABOVE: Dashes of vivid tile surrounding the entry to the courtyard give only a hint of what awaits visitors inside this tiny house in a comfortable San Gabriel Valley neighborhood.

Although Pasadena is renowned for its rambling mansions and the world's finest collection of Greene and Greene Craftsman-style homes, it also is the site of thousands of bungalows and cottages built in the teens, twenties, and thirties. These tiny homes were the pride of families who couldn't resist the lure of the beautiful San Gabriel Mountains and the vast valley below them, yet couldn't afford the grand scale mansions in tonier neighborhoods.

Many of these modest residences are clustered near Pasadena City College and the prestigious California Institute of Technology. One of them, an intimate 1930s duplex, features a collage of stained and textured glass that makes colors dance throughout the interior. Its owner, interior designer Van-Martin Rowe, says he eschewed curtains to allow refracted light to change the look and mood of each room. "Layering textures and colors of glass in the room results in constant surprises," he notes. "The light in the room rarely looks the same twice." More than thirty-two patterns are etched into the windowpanes scattered

throughout the house. The swirling colored panes were manufactured by the Judson Studios, a stained-glass works, founded more than a hundred years ago in Pasadena's Arroyo Seco area, which was the major source of glass for architects Frank Lloyd Wright and the brothers Greene.

But Rowe's use of color goes beyond tinkering with light and glass. The designer also painted a continuous "horizon line" on the walls throughout the house to make each room's eight-foot ceiling seem higher. To amplify the effect, he painted trompe l'oeil coves on each ceiling, selecting different "sky" hues for each room: a golden morning glow in the east-facing living room, a vibrant blue afternoon hue in the den, with its large corner windows, and a deep purple night shade in the bedroom.

Against the backdrop of these cleverly painted rooms, Rowe displays varied textures of old and new wicker, fabrics garnered from Europe, Mexico, and Guatemala, and fanciful collectibles. On the newly constructed front courtyard, he displays potted plants and flowers. Ten months of the year, the front door is open and this diminutive indoor-outdoor space becomes an extension of his living room. More important, however, the space adds some architectural complexity to what was a nondescript little bungalow.

LEFT: In the sunny sitting room, a white wicker lamp with Victorian fringe lights the taupe wall. A handmade picture frame and trinket box encrusted with seashells from Maui are Rowe's reference to living "just a freeway away from the beach." The designer styled the wooden tulip-and-vase sculpture.

LEFT: A dozen years of valentines, lovingly surrounded with ribbons and lace, are assembled and framed as a colorful and very personal art form in the dining room. The delicate English Beswick pitcher with curving palm-tree handle is from the 1930s. BELOW, MIDDLE: This mirror, ringed with masses of aniline-dyed Guatemalan corn-husk flowers, reflects ribbons of paint in the bedroom. Oaxacan ce- ramic angels, purchased from vendors on Olvera Street in the heart of Los Angeles's original Plaza, add their own blessing to the display. **BELOW: Panes of stained glass create a patchwork backdrop for a turn-of-the-century glass panel entitled "The Tortoise and Hare" in the dining-room window. Rowe has arranged wicker chairs around a table draped with Guatemalan ikat fabric. On** the Victorian tortoise-bamboo cabinet, another two-dimensional wooden floral sculpture designed by Rowe and a pair of painted wood cats add a whimsical touch. **LEFT: Pillows made from South American shopping satchels are arranged with chenille-embroidered kitty and pup pillows on a casually draped sofa. The hand-painted table is inset with Catalina tiles. The faux coving at the ceiling is an effect created solely with paint.**

WARNER / GARRICK HOUSE

This house could have remained a plain white fifties "ranchburger," like the rest of the flat-roofed, one-story ranch-style homes that line many a city block here. But to artist Laurie Lee Warner and filmmaker Eddie Garrick, the small Laurel Canyon house acted as a blank canvas. This aesthetically uninhibited couple chose a palette of uncompromisingly strong shades—more than twenty in all—and painted the exterior in vivid asymmetrical blocks. When the sun is at full strength, the building shimmers like a stained-glass window.

Inside, the collage of color is no less startling. Ethnic, primitive, and folk art from around the world tells the story of two people's travels in living color. Warner and Garrick fearlessly break all the rules of traditional design. To their delight, textiles, pottery glazes, and stained glass from various periods clash on walls, floors, and furnishings. Add an apple-green vase with amethyst irises and some kumquat branches from the garden and the effect is electrifying.

Even Warner's wardrobe is wearable art. Her passion for color shows up in her inventive personal style. Hot-colored ethnic clothing, multi-hued cowboy boots, antique beaded handbags, and turquoise and coral Native American jewelry are part of her image. And, not surprisingly, her flamboyant apparel is incorporated into the decor.

BELOW: A miniature wooden canoe carved in the early 1900s, like those of the Indians from the Pacific Northwest, is suspended in a window overlooking a fruit-laden kumquat tree in the garden. **BOTTOM: Welcoming visitors on the front porch are cacti potted in Warner's hand-painted containers. Just inside the** front door is a quirky garage-sale cowboy floor lamp. The couch is covered with bright patterned blankets and a well-worn Indian-head pillow.

BELOW LEFT: In Warner's atelier, the painted barrel cactus chair is one of many examples of her own functional art. A Hawaiian grass skirt hung at the window helps to diffuse the sun's intense rays. For inspiration, the artist surrounds herself with amusing found objects, family photographs, and the tools of her trade, myriad tubes of acrylic paint. Her signature strokes can even be found on the television set. ABOVE: On Warner's bedroom dresser, a coral branch forms a unique display piece for her Indian and Mexican jewelry. RIGHT: The graphic linoleum floor, designed by Ty Ross, is art meant to be walked upon. The artist interpreted the vivid designs that appear on Warner's collection of colorful cowboy boots. More shots of color are provided by the stacks of Metlox plates and Mexican cactus wineglasses in the cabinet and by English majolica, Mexican pottery, and the works of local folk artists on the counters.

LEFT: The log-cabin-motif dresser in the bedroom is part of a complete set that Garrick's parents bought at Sears Roebuck in the forties. On top are baskets and trays filled with jewelry and trinkets. On the floor, a lineup of cowboy boots is in keeping with the room's western theme. BELOW: A Mexican tin gecko watches over the maple bed, ablaze with prints upon prints. Dozens of souvenir "snowies," mostly with Los Angeles themes, adorn the windowsill.

LEFT: Sunlight casts an afternoon glow on this Pennsylvania oak-and-hickory rocking chair and footstool. The wood and papier-mâché screen depicting a bullfight is from Mexico. Outside, the garden is brightened with one of Warner's prickly cactus sculptures in painted wood. RIGHT: Warner inherited her grandmother's antique beaded handbags, each with a copper penny inside, and today they decorate a wall in the artist's workroom.

With waves of newcomers arriving in the city throughout the twentieth century, a significant percentage of the Los Angeles population has been

Mass Movements

transient and in immediate need of a place to call home—at least temporarily. Unlike residents of other big cities, Angelenos fill a short-term need—until a job is found or a screenplay is sold and there's enough money to buy a house with some land, the ultimate dream.

5

LEFT: Built as a Norman-style apartment house in 1928, Château Marmont, designed by Arnold Weitzman, became an apartment-hotel almost immediately thereafter and later a full-fledged hotel. Strategically located above Sunset Strip at the foot of the Hollywood Hills, the chateau has always attracted movie actors, screenwriters, and directors. **BELOW:** Apartments in Los Angeles are wrapped in all kinds of packages, both elegant and quirky. This ship-shaped building is located, not surprisingly, a few steps from the Pacific. **ABOVE RIGHT:** The Villa d'Este apartments, designed by Pierpont and Walter S. Davis in 1928, exemplify the lavish design characteristic of the twenties. The building was inspired by its namesake in Italy.

Even so, there's always been a premium on aesthetically appealing apartments. Complexes have varied dramatically in style, size, and shape over the years, partly in response to fashion but also in response to land prices, construction

costs, building codes, and the types of tenants for whom they were intended. Apartments come dressed as turreted French chateaux, quaint Bavarian villages, and great marble edifices. They can wrap around swimming pools, straddle parking garages, rise heavenward, climb hillsides, or spread out horizontally unit by unit. Arguably, some building types have met with more success than others in pleasing the eye and capitalizing on the city's temperate climate and abundant vegetation.

As important as comfort and visual appeal is a building's sense of community. In a metropolis with no social or physical hub, the ability to provide residents with a communal environment provides reason enough to move in. Some buildings have four units, some house a thousand, but the concept is the same.

After the turn of the century, clusters of Craftsman bungalows, such as Arthur and Alfred Heineman's Bowen Court in Pasadena (1910), provided ideal ready-made neighborhoods for retirees, vacationers, and young families arriving from the Midwest. Spaced across still-inexpensive

ABOVE: Newcomers from points east typically found shelter in bungalow courtyard complexes such as this one, circa 1920. The prevailing aesthetic stressed access to gardens as well as a sense of community. BELOW: The enclosed courtyard at the Mexican-style Villa Primavera, designed by Arthur and Nina Zwebell in 1923, continues to be a peaceful and fanciful urban refuge. Here, the outside staircase is defined by a *campanario* minus a bell.

land, bungalow courts consisted of small attached or freestanding houses with porches and gardens that faced each other across tree-lined walkways rather than across noisy streets. The Heinemans' Bowen Court even offered its own log teahouse. Sadly, few bungalow courts stand today, doomed as white elephants in a time when cost-efficient, high-density housing is now the aim of most developers.

Courtyard apartments, a close relative of the bungalow courts, became perhaps the city's most delightful rendition of apartment living. In 1910, Irving Gill applied his then-progressive fusion of Spanish shapes and clean modern lines to apartment complexes. His Lewis Courts in Sierra Madre overlook landscaped terraces, while the Horatio West Court, in Santa Monica (1921), contains a small patio and is just a block from the Pacific Ocean. The Horatio West Court is one of the few early courtyard apartment complexes to have been completely refurbished and converted to privately owned townhouses.

Arthur Zwebell and his wife, Nina Wilcox Zwebell, built some of the finest Spanish Colonial Revival courtyard apartments the city has known, most of them located in Hollywood and catering to people working in the movie business. Not an architect by profession, Arthur was the contractor and designer. Nina was responsible for interior decoration and eventually op-

erated a furniture factory to provide the buildings with appropriate Mediterranean-style appointments. Influenced by Andalusian, Mexican, and, on occasion, Moorish architecture, their plans were elegantly simple, with an eye for detail. Sombrero-shaped terra-cotta flowerpots still hang from the walls of the Zwebells' Andalusia (1926), which is approached through an attractive forecourt for automobiles.

There were many other designers of apartment courts, including architects and brothers F. Pierpont Davis and Walter S. Davis, who planned Villa d'Este (1926) and the Roman Gardens (1928). The Depression considerably slowed apartment construction, although the last major Spanish-style courtyard apartment complex of this period, Hollywood's El Cadiz, designed by Milton J. Black, was completed in 1936, according to the definitive book on the subject, *Courtyard Housing in Los Angeles*, by Stefanos Polyzoides, Roger Sherwood, and James Tice.

Not all 1920s and 1930s apartment buildings had courtyards, however. Hundreds of two-story Spanish-style apartments were built, swathed in white stucco and crowned with tile roofs. Access to the second floor was often provided by an outdoor stairway edged with wrought-iron railing. In several neighborhoods, city

ABOVE, FAR LEFT: For designers Arthur and Nina Zwebell, the courtyard concept was essential to the vitality of apartment living. Inside the courtyard at their Casa Laguna (see page 147), strong colors create a sense of otherworldliness. **ABOVE LEFT:** Hundreds of Spanish-style apartments sprouted across the city throughout the twenties. Even those without architectural pedigree feature such romantic effects as balconies overflowing with bougainvillea. **RIGHT:** Passing under the vaulted ceilings at Villa d'Este in West Hollywood transports residents into another realm. **FAR RIGHT:** Lush tropical landscaping and decorative tile, such as that seen at the entrance to Villa d'Este, are hallmarks of 1920s apartment design, still enjoyed today.

blocks are still lined with these buildings, as their charm endures.

By the mid-1920s, when the population of greater Los Angeles passed one million, large luxury buildings, some eight stories high, were also being erected, including the Rex Arms, the Arcady, the Westonia, and the French-style Chateau Marmont, above the Sunset Strip. Ready to provide the good life, some of these "high-class" buildings even had ballrooms and banquet rooms. Residents could walk into furnished units equipped with a full supply of cooking utensils, linens, and housewares. The Rex Arms stocked each unit with china, silverware, and stemware for six, including goblets, champagne glasses, and finger bowls. The idea was to create an instant middle-to-upper-middle-class iden-

tity for newly minted Angelenos. More modest two- and three-story buildings popped up as well, some dressed in inventive packages, such as the popular Egyptian Revival motif.

In the thirties, the Streamline Moderne style—epitomized by curved walls, glass brick, and ocean-liner "porthole" windows—emerged not only on all manner of commercial structures and hotels but

also on duplex houses (dwellings with separate apartments for two families) and apartments across the city. It was a less ornate, less expensive rendition of the glitzier art deco style, which didn't have much impact on residential design here other than on the spectacular Sunset Tower apartments, now the St. James Club, designed by Leland A. Bryant (1929). The forms borrowed from Streamline Moderne made sense for developers in difficult economic times. However, cost cutting stopped when it came to built-in interior amenities such as dinettes, desks, and cabinets, which added to the comfort and charm of the apartments and made them easy to inhabit.

At the same time, the city's key Modernist architects took up the challenge of designing affordable multifamily housing. Richard J. Neutra's eight-unit Strathmore Apartments (1937) in Westwood is a rendition of the then-contemporary Interna-

ABOVE LEFT: Ted Tokio Tanaka designed a modern version of an early L.A. courtyard-apartment complex in 1987. His Flower Apartment building in Venice is painted in a pleasing palette of floral colors. ABOVE: The Falk Apartments, designed by Rudolph M. Schindler, were an early-modernist take on L.A. living. The building's asymmetrical blocks were an avant-garde departure from the vernacular Spanish courtyard buildings of the twenties and thirties. RIGHT: The Electric Art Block in Venice (see page 161) addresses the contemporary challenges of apartment living. It is meant to merge stylistically with other buildings in an industrial zone near the beach.

tional Style yet still was planned around a central garden like the Spanish-style buildings that preceded it. Neutra's contemporary, Rudolph M. Schindler, built more than a dozen apartments and duplex houses, including Silver Lake's Falk Apartments (1939), in which each of the hillside units has its own terrace and view. Gregory Ain's cubistic Dunsmuir Apartments (1937), which scales a hillside in Baldwin Hills, also provides each of its four units with access to a private patio.

Following World War II, L.A.'s notorious "dingbat" era in apartments began. The appellation, thought to be coined by a UCLA professor who lived in one, refers to the scores of nondescript two- and three-story geometric structures that went up quickly and cheaply all over the city to accommodate the millions of new arrivals. To exploit land to the fullest, the buildings often perched over unsightly garages that were open to the street. Decorative embellishments were reduced to a minimum, and included tacked-on starburst light fixtures or large, futuristic lettering that spelled the building's grandiose name—La Linda, Champagne Garden, King's Arms.

Styles changed in the 1960s and 1970s, when developers undertook massive 600- to 1000-unit apartment complexes with an emphasis on landscaping and community. Facilities such as tennis courts, gyms, pools, Jacuzzis, and elaborate clubhouses were included to help ease a sense of alienation felt by newcomers. Typical of these "garden apartments" is the 981-unit Mariners

Village in Marina del Rey, designed by Kamnitzer and Marks (1971). A 23-acre complex with winding cobblestone paths, bridges, and man-made waterfalls, it features buildings designed in the "marine style," using nautical lanterns and wooden posts and pilings to make each building appear as though it sits at the end of a pier.

Although there had been "emotional resistance" in Los Angeles to high-rise apartments, the thirteen-story luxury Wilshire Terrace cooperative, designed by Peter Kamnitzer for Victor Gruen Associ-

ates in 1959, was one of the first of many more such buildings to come. Today, the stretch of Wilshire Boulevard between Beverly Hills and Westwood Village is a golden ghetto of expensive condominium towers that were built in the eighties, their lobbies lined with marble and terrazzo. Rich foreign investors, movie stars, and well-to-do Angelenos who left behind sumptuous homes in Bel-Air because they no longer wanted to bother with upkeep opted for low-maintenance, high-security condo life. This so-called new era of luxury reached its apex with the Wilshire House (1982), designed by Gruen Associates, which boasted two $10-million, 7000-square-foot penthouses.

As real estate prices continued to skyrocket in the eighties, condominium complexes of various sizes, largely devoid of architectural distinction, sprouted across the city, from the ocean to the San Fernando Valley. Suddenly, everyone wanted to own real estate, no matter how small. Existing apartments were being converted into condos; everyone wanted a piece of the action.

Today, a few young architects of distinction are taking an interest in apartment design. In the last few years, Koning Eizenberg Architecture—Australian husband-and-wife transplants Hank Koning and Julie Eizenberg—and Ted Tokio Tanaka, a Tokyo native now living here, have made stylish statements on small buildings in Venice and Santa Monica. These contemporary architects are infusing buildings with color and energy. And recalling the lessons of L.A.'s apartments of the past, they are integrating interior spaces with modern outdoor courtyards and gardens.

CASA LAGUNA

FAR LEFT: The husband-and-wife design team of Arthur and Nina Zwebell always employed romantic architectural features, such as the row of columns at one edge of the courtyard of this apartment complex in the Los Feliz district. LEFT: Inside the courtyard, the original tiled fountain continues to serve as the building's centerpiece and gathering place. To the right is an exterior fireplace, a typical Zwebell touch. The square courtyard, which is completely shielded from the street, has a sense of quiet and privacy. BELOW LEFT: The streetside view of the building is of a two-story loggia with old-world carved-wood detailing.

Only the deep ocher hue of this corner apartment building hints at the beauty that lies just inside the gate. Casa Laguna was built in 1928 by two of the city's premier courtyard-apartment designers, Arthur and Nina Wilcox Zwebell. A year later, with the crash of Wall Street and the downturn in construction, the Zwebells left the profession, ending a brief career that contributed much to the architecture of the city.

Like the Zwebells' other apartment complexes, Casa Laguna is distinguished by the lovely design of its fountain, gardens, and central courtyard. In a densely populated neighborhood such as this one, a sense of quiet and privacy becomes even more valuable. Some of the details worth noticing are the multicolored tile work, the carved wood balustrades and columns, and the newly planted drought-resistant garden.

A tasteful mix of Mexican antiques and contemporary conceptual art complement the architecture of one of the largest apartments, pictured here, amplifying its sense of history while bringing it into the present tense.

UN COHETE DE SEÑALES   ENCENDIDO SOBRE UNA FRONTERA

LEFT: The art collector who lives here has made original use of the high ceilings. He translated into Spanish the words of the New York and Amsterdam conceptual artist Lawrence Weiner and hired a sign painter to install them overhead. In English they read: "A flare ignited upon a boundary." The iron chandelier is original to the building. BELOW: In the bedroom, the wooden bed was designed by Michael Tracy. Figures on the nineteenth-century American trunk include Mexican crosses and a Brazilian doll.

ABOVE: The vividly tiled bathroom counter holds mementos and more art pieces.

ABOVE: The Zwebells created drama in each apartment unit they designed, particularly those with high beamed ceilings and eye-catching corner fireplaces, such as the one shown here. A kilim rug and antique furnishings are juxtaposed with contemporary art pieces in the living room, including a gridlike chair designed by Michael Tracy. The sculpture on the table at the right is by John Chamberlain, and the photographs on the back wall are by Rudolf Schwarzkogler. A Fulper pot and a Japanese vase are displayed on a small Craftsman-period wooden bar, all of which belonged to the owner's family.

BRADY APARTMENT

FAR LEFT: The cheery kitchen of Tad Brady's apartment was refurbished for improved function as well as to include appropriate 1930s details. At one end of the checkerboard linoleum floor is a built-in red vinyl booth and Formica table, the ideal spot to sip a cup of java. ABOVE: Brady recently added a glass-brick wall when restoring the duplex. BELOW LEFT: Brady's property looks out over the Franklin Avenue Bridge, designed by J. C. Wright and affectionately known as the Shakespeare Bridge because of its quirky Gothic towers. Built in 1926, it is surely one of L.A.'s more exotic sights.

This small duplex house is defined by the clean forms of the once popular Streamline Moderne, a thirties style that emerged from the new machine aesthetic and widespread interest in aerodynamic forms. Still a little jewel, it is immaculately preserved in a neighborhood of Los Angeles that lured its most adventurous architects, including Rudolph M. Schindler, Raphael Soriano, and Lloyd Wright. Designed by Wesley Eager in 1937, the building is all curving surfaces, rounded corners, glass blocks, and mirrors. Interiors were designed to harmonize with the machine-age exterior forms.

Tad Brady, who owns the building and lives in the upstairs unit, has maintained its original character with furniture and decorative objects of the period, from his chrome Osterizer blender to his Fiesta pottery. Large expanses of windows are covered with the wide-slatted venetian blinds so typical of the 1930s. The owner was born long after his apartment house was built, yet clearly sympathizes with its Moderne sensibilities.

LEFT: The blue-tinted mirrors and built-in desk are original to the living room, as are the black glass tiles on the fireplace surround. The curves of the streamlined chrome-and-leather armchairs, designed by Los Angeles architect Kem Weber, mimic the bends on the railings on the front of the house. The contemporary steel side table was designed by Los Angeles designer Bob Jos-

ten. BELOW: Departing from the 1930s theme, the bedroom is dominated by a contemporary futon, while the towers of the Shakespeare Bridge outside appear to form a headboard. The pastel drawing of Los Angeles is by Pam Rossi. RIGHT: A classic Streamline Moderne porthole illuminates a built-in cabinet in the entry hall. The panther print is from the thirties.

ABOVE: Even a potted schefflera tree has a curving trunk. A poster made for Pasadena's annual Doo-Dah Parade hangs behind it in the hallway.

MURPHY APARTMENT

ABOVE: The corner view of the Sovereign shows the regal stature of this Santa Monica landmark. Located just a short walk from vast Santa Monica beach and its historic pier, the building has many units reserved as residences for year-round tenants, while several designated suites remain available for travelers from all over the world. Murphy's apartment is the corner unit with an orange tree on its balcony.

LEFT: Artwork by some of Los Angeles's most well-known artists, including Charles Arnoldi, Billy Al Bengston, and Ed Ruscha, lines the entry hall to the offbeat apartment of architectural designer Brian A. Murphy, whose home is a direct reflection of his varied interests and athletic pursuits. He designed the entry table from baseball bats and created his own shrine, capped with an image of Jesus silk-screened on a Fruit of the Loom T-shirt. Two pairs of swim fins, which he often employs, pay homage to his love of the beach. RIGHT: The legendary San Francisco—based architect Julia Morgan, who was renowned for her romantic Mediterranean approach to design, situated a balcony directly above the double entry doors of the Sovereign Hotel. Another Morgan touch is a large walled courtyard garden, which makes the main entrance to the hotel apartments seem even grander.

An architectural designer who has created some of Los Angeles's most talked-about residences, Brian A. Murphy is a master of found objects. He sees to it that every project he completes for his adventurous clients, many in the entertainment business, is on the cutting edge of accepted design. He incorporates inexpensive everyday objects—including wrought-iron grates, hay bales, and clay flowerpots—into formal elements of style.

His own constantly changing apartment is a test lab for his latest ideas. He lives in the Sovereign Hotel in Santa Monica, a Spanish Colonial Revival building designed by Julia Morgan and located a few blocks from the ocean. At the time this apartment was photographed, he was playing around with Jackson Pollock–like paint splatters on his living-room rug; a few weeks later, the rug came up, and he painted the wood floor high-gloss white. Murphy also paid a visit to Pasadena's famous Rose Bowl flea market, where he bought even more offbeat furniture and accessories.

What never changes is Murphy's affection for the outdoors. The main seating in his living room is a large semicircular garden bench that one might expect to see in a park rather than in a small apartment. It's offset by a formal chaise longue covered in red satin damask.

The Southern California native, who spent many summers as a lifeguard, is a confirmed surfer. The corner in which Murphy props his surfboard is more than a convenient storage space—its position allows him to sit and admire the board as an art form. More conventional Los Angeles art lines the entranceway, along with Murphy's swim fins, which he can grab when he spies the perfect wave.

ABOVE: At night, Murphy prefers the glimmer of candlelight to anything electricity can provide. He lines the perimeter of the living room with dozens of multicolored votive candles to create a festive mood. **RIGHT:** Improvisation is Murphy's byword. In the dining room, rather than opt for a conventional table, the designer transformed ordinary objects into something extraordinary. Coiled steel, a baseball bat, and decorative window grating, all coated with white baked enamel, become a conversation piece as well as a place to dine. The bouquet of tulips is gathered in a free-form vase shaped from blocks of plate glass.

ABOVE: Murphy says he positioned his bed for an unobstructed view of the ocean, and no curtains inhibit the panorama of sand, palms, and the Pacific. For quick spins on the oceanside bicycle path, Murphy's wheels are within easy reach. **RIGHT:** When Murphy tired of his living-room carpet, he recolored it rather than replace it, using what he calls "a potent porridge" of black, brown, red, and purple Rit dye. A semicircular park bench and a French chaise longue covered in damask surround the baled-twig coffee table. A tin chair from India and Murphy's surfboard add the final touches.

BELOW: Rusted saw blades are perched on eucalyptus branches to form end tables in the conversation area of the revised living room. The seats of both the bench and the chair have been covered in AstroTurf for an outdoorsy approach to indoor living. The coffee table is composed of a stainless-steel barbecue grill supported by a terra-cotta flowerpot. Murphy's ingenuity turned five eucalyptus boughs into wall sculpture. On view in the hall is a painting by Los Angeles artist Jim Ganzer. The palm tree image is by Murphy. RIGHT: A molded plastic shelf with baroque details supports another Murphy still life. On top of the shelf he places a water glass filled to overflowing with daisies from the Sovereign garden. The faux transistor radio and camera are actually blocks of pine handpainted by the designer. FAR RIGHT: Murphy's design ideas never stop, and his tableaux reflect his nonstop creativity. Here, a free-form grouping, including an easel, empty frames, and a few gilt-edged mirrors, are lit by votive candles.

ELECTRIC ART BLOCK

FAR LEFT: In artist Terrell Moore's workout room, the lines of his Flex Cross Training System machine are not unlike those seen in his painting entitled "Crucifixion." LEFT: A curve in a wall fronting one side of the Electric Art Block apartment complex, designed by architects Hank Koning, Julie Eizenberg, and Glenn Robert Erikson, has a nautical theme—it seems to echo the shape of a whale or the waves of the nearby Pacific. Many small windows were employed to take advantage of the ocean breezes and create natural ventilation. Angled steel pipes provide gritty decorative detail. BELOW LEFT: Seen from one end, the apartment building could easily be mistaken for an industrial complex. The skewed angles of a stucco trapezoid create a striking focal point beside a zigzagging staircase.

The Electric Art Block, so named for its street location on Electric Avenue and the profession of its tenants, is a twenty-unit artists' loft building located on a narrow strip of land where streetcars once operated in Venice. For the last decade, the community has been enjoying a renaissance of building and the arts, and this fascinating building is one of the architectural surprises.

Composed of five stucco blocks joined by angled walls of sheet metal and glass, the Art Block easily blends into the surrounding commercial neighborhood, which houses many artists' studios with less interesting blueprints. The use of bright colors, decorative pipe columns, and chain-link mesh instantly distinguishes it from other buildings in this industrial zone, a few blocks from popular Venice Beach.

The building was designed by Koning Eizenberg Architecture, Inc., with Glenn Robert Erikson. Hank Koning and Julie Eizenberg came to Los Angeles from Melbourne, Australia, and quickly made a mark on the architectural scene in the city. The pair has been responsible for several apartment buildings in Santa Monica and is designing an expansion to Farmers Market, the legendary Los Angeles tourist stop.

The dramatic, uninterrupted spaces in Art Block lofts appealed to Dallas transplant Terrell Moore, whose huge Abstract Expressionist paintings demand large walls. His minimal furnishings have a sense of rawness suitable to this austere environment. Indeed, the only designer label here appears on the artist's cross-training exercise machine.

ABOVE: In the bedroom, a triptych of tree images painted by Moore dominates one wall. The only color in the room comes from the faux brick wall, which Moore painted in order to create a fabric "curtain" to conceal his personal gym. In front of a muslin-draped couch, a plank of wood supported by glass bricks becomes a coffee table. On display is a pair of wood pears made by Tom Cook, a Dallas-based artist. ABOVE LEFT: Even life's basic necessities have been taken over by Moore's artistic vision. He applied graffiti-like strokes to his low-tech refrigerator but left the digital clock as it was.

LEFT: Viewed from the second-floor loft/kitchen is Moore's painting studio/gallery, which is filled with his large canvases, many of them covered with roof tar, alkyd, enamels, wood stain, and varnishes. ABOVE: Moore celebrates the Spartan in his bedroom, where he bypassed carpeting in favor of the raw wood floors. The minimal arrangement of furniture and black-and-white art in the third-floor room maintains the art gallery feeling. The diptych over the bed is echoed in the shape of a side table, also by Moore.

City of Angels

It's possible to take the name Los Angeles quite literally. If ever there was a place where individuals could spread their wings in search of spiritual truth, surely it is the City of Angels.

The city's inherently tolerant culture invites inhabitants to express their beliefs however they please. Unencumbered by rigid, long-standing religious tradition, L.A. has become an important spiritual center for

established religions as well as a prime territory for new spiritual movements, fads, and cults. Signs of these diverse faiths are evident not just in ecclesiastical buildings but

LEFT: The elaborate interior of St. Sophia Greek Orthodox Cathedral, designed by architects Gus Kalionzes, Charles Klingerman, and Albert Walker, displays the beautiful murals painted by William Chavalas, the primary artist. Chavalas, who worked at the 20th Century Fox studio, painted almost all the artwork on canvas on the movie lot and then transferred it to the walls of the church. **TOP:** An angelic bracket in the loft home of Michael Hack-

ett (see page 191), bearing the faces of two angels, holds a coral branch. **ABOVE RIGHT:** Among the more delightful religious buildings that can be seen in the city is the Taj Mahal look-alike Vedanta Temple, with three onion domes and the sacred om symbol above the entrance. It's located near the Hollywood Freeway in Hollywood. The Vedanta Society of Southern California is part of the Ramakrishna Order of India.

6

also in the most unexpected public places—on billboards, at bus stops, and painted on the sides of trucks. Perhaps that makes people feel free to imbue their private homes with sacred symbols in unconventional ways, as seen in the residences pictured here. Some people express their spiritual inspirations in the architecture of their dwellings. Others simply appreciate and surround themselves with the beauty of religious icons or the mystical quality of crystals.

With its history of fluid growth, Los Angeles has never been a community with a fixed religious establishment, so spiritual

pluralism can flourish. Although prejudice and problems certainly exist, newcomers here are welcome to find their place in the sun. Since the city was founded, most new Angelenos have been able to find the same churches they left back home—if the institutions weren't here, they established them. Today, with more than two thousand places of worship in the city, dozens of faiths coexist.

However, many newcomers transplanted their belongings but cast off their religious ties in search of alternatives.

BELOW LEFT: Spirituality enters into the design of many Angelenos' homes. At the residence known as Casa Pequeña (see page 177), the owner has built niches to accommodate a pair of Portuguese angels, circa 1600. **BELOW:** At the home of Zalman King and Patricia Louisiana Knop (see page 197), large-scale *santo* figures are positioned throughout the house, including this one on the mantel of a bedroom fireplace.

Whether they were seeking a sense of community or spiritual shelter in this unconventional new world, the answer for many didn't exist in conventional religion. They were ripe for offbeat philosophy.

As early as 1840—just after the missions were secularized—the first documented religious cult took hold in Southern California. It was led by a Scotsman aptly named William Money, who was convinced that his mission from Christ was to spread the word of a New Age and that he was told to begin in Los Angeles. A faith leader and persuasive speaker who was versed in multiple theologies, Money and his Reformed New Testament Church of the Faith of Jesus Christ took root in the pueblo, much to the dismay of the padres. As he healed more and more uneducated Mexicans and Indians, they eventually turned to him as their leader and provided him with enough money to erect an eight-sided building in San Gabriel, not far from the mission. Money died in 1880, leaving no successor to lead his church, and it soon faded into obscurity.

From 1900 to 1920, theosophy (the

ABOVE: In the West Los Angeles home of Kristin Glover and Cary Weiss, a meditation-and-reading room contains a collage of religious objects, books, and a touch of the mystic. Here, Glover lights candles and ponders meaningful photographs, Buddhas, and Christian symbols.

practice of contemplation or revelation to make mystical contact with the divine) and New Thought (a New England religious philosophy that emphasized the power of the mind in achieving health and happiness) took hold in Southern California, setting the stage for dozens of cults and esoteric societies to develop. Certainly the health-food advocates, metaphysical thinkers, and nudist camps that thrived in the twenties and thirties and continue to flourish today have contributed to the quirky, eccentric image of the City of Angels.

Many spiritual movements have left a visual imprint on the city. Without question the most powerful influence came from the Franciscan missions. But other ecclesiastical buildings have also become landmarks throughout the city, including St. Vibiana's Catholic Cathedral downtown (1876), with

ABOVE: Interpretations of spirituality appear in different forums, both public and private, throughout the city. A mixed-media shrine to Our Lady of Guadalupe was built in stages in the late 1980s by Eduardo Oropeza in the parking lot of Self-Help Graphics, a nonprofit arts organization based in East Los Angeles. ABOVE RIGHT: Gracing the home office of Claudia James and Peter Bartlett (see page 187) is an articulated Guatemalan angel from the mid-nineteenth century. It is flanked by turn-of-the-century American mercury glass vases. **RIGHT: Bottle caps enter the world of the sacred in this contemporary folk-art crucifix hanging in the entry hall of a private home.**

its Baroque-inspired Italianate façade; the Nishi Hongwanji Buddhist Temple (1925), an unusual blend of Oriental and Egyptian decoration; Vedanta Temple (1938), which has been likened to the Taj Mahal; the towering Church of Jesus Christ of Latter-Day Saints Temple (1955), with the golden angel Moroni at its apex; and the redwood-and-glass Wayfarer's Chapel (1951) at Portuguese Bend, the most famous work of Lloyd Wright's.

The largesse of the entertainment industry figured importantly in two of the city's loveliest places of worship. The War-

ner brothers—Jack, Harry, and Albert—hired Hugo Ballin, an art director at their studio, to paint the dramatic murals inside the domed sanctuary of the Wilshire Boulevard Temple (1929). Louis B. Mayer donated the stained-glass windows, and Irving Thalberg provided the painted decorative motifs inside the dome. Nearby, at St. Sophia Greek Orthodox Cathedral (1952), another film mogul, Charles Skouras, engaged artists from 20th Century Fox to paint the entire building, including its huge canvas murals.

Alternative sects have had their impact on the cityscape too. In 1911, the now-

ABOVE LEFT: The eastern lunette at Wilshire Boulevard Temple represents prophets, priests, and rabbis. In the center is a monumental Moses, from whose head emanate rays of light.
ABOVE: The architects of the Byzantine-style temple were A. M. Edelman, S. Tilden Norton, and David C. Allison.

RIGHT: Seen here singing as she plays her piano, evangelist Aimee Semple McPherson of the Angelus Temple had undeniable star quality. The onetime minister's wife also lived like a star, with a fancy car and a large house.

defunct Krotona colony—home to an off-beat metaphysical movement—was housed on a 15-acre spread in Hollywood, complete with a lotus pond and a Moorish-Egyptian temple. The outdoor theatrical productions at its amphitheater have been credited as the model for the world-renowned Hollywood Bowl alfresco programs. Paramahansa Yogananda's Self-Realization Shrine (1950), on the west end of Sunset Boulevard, plants an impressive East Indian paradise—golden domes, a swan-filled lake, a shrine to Gandhi, and a huge meditation garden—in the middle of suburban Pacific Palisades. It's difficult to overlook L. Ron Hubbard's Church of Scientology, with its many buildings, storefronts, and billboards splashed throughout the city, including an enormous celestial blue complex in the heart of Hollywood with a flashing electronic billboard.

But no monument to New Age religion carries a history as fabled as the Angelus Temple in Echo Park—the temple that the legendary Sister Aimee Semple McPherson built. A former Salvation Army soldier, Sister Aimee brought her Foursquare Gospel to Southern California in 1918. In less than five years her message of faith, healing, Second Coming, and redemption, coupled with outrageous theatrics in the pulpit and on the airwaves (she was the city's third radio

evangelist), would make her the high priestess of Southern California's organized religion. She preached to standing-room-only crowds in the 4300-seat Angelus Temple, which she erected with $1.5 million collected from her followers across the United States and Australia. When it was completed in 1925, it was the largest church in America. After she orchestrated her own kidnapping and was then involved in a much-publicized sex scandal, Sister Aimee's influence waned; she eventually died of an overdose of sleeping pills in 1945. But her temple, which looks like a cross between a Roman sports arena and the Mormon Tabernacle in Salt Lake City, is still in use by the International Church of the Foursquare Gospel.

Still, some of the city's most spiritually inspired environments are individual residences. In a way, some people regard their homes as their own private temples. In the City of Angels, all kinds have a place.

BELOW: So popular was the sentiment for California missions that houses across the city were built with architectural details that evoked them. This private residence, built in Santa Monica in the 1930s, exhibits rounded parapets and a tower. ABOVE RIGHT: Moving vignettes of religious statuary are seen throughout the extraordinary King/Knop

House (see page 197). In an upstairs bedroom, a carved wooden *santo* figure and an angel stand on a tile-inlaid table. RIGHT: Simple yet colorful shrines, such as this one dedicated to the Virgin Mary, can be spotted among the shops and restaurants on Olvera Street in the city's historic Plaza area.

ABBEY SAN ENCINO

Abbey San Encino was the name given to the home of the early Los Angeles intellectual and printer Clyde Browne. Browne was intent on building a home that was more than just four walls and a roof, a place that reflected his fascination with California's old Spanish missions. In 1909, he began work on the house in the Highland Park region of Los Angeles, building it by hand of redwood and the indigenous boulders from the nearby Arroyo Seco. Amazingly, his handiwork has withstood several severe earthquakes centered not far from the imposing building.

The structure is part California mission, with its rhythmic, rounded arches, its tiled roof, its bell tower, modeled after the one at Mission San Carlos Borromeo de Carmelo in Carmel (1797), its grape-vine-covered patio, and a long, narrow chapel complete with pipe organ and

choir loft. It is also part medieval castle, with a dank dungeon in the basement and massive iron door locks brought over from European castles. In addition to housing Browne and his family, the Abbey also served as his printing studio, which produced most of the brochures, publications, and yearbooks of Occidental College. For his workroom, Browne commissioned the nearby Judson Studios to create a round stained-glass window depicting a friar and a Native American at a printing press.

Much of the furniture was carved by Browne himself and still remains in the house today. Browne died in his Abbey in 1941 and his descendants continue to own it. Today, the structure is surrounded by a prized cactus-and-succulent garden, and is located just a few blocks from the roaring Pasadena Freeway. But the churchlike serenity intended by the elder Browne remains firmly intact.

RIGHT: An extensive collection of California's Franciscan dishes in the classic Desert Rose pattern is a colorful addition to the small dining room. On the wall, a commemorative poster, now faded with age, celebrates one of Southern California's time-honored traditions, the Pasadena Tournament of Roses Parade. FAR RIGHT: Browne carved all the wood detailing on the massive pipe organ that dominates one end of the "chapel," which serves as the house's living room. Made by the Los Angeles–based Angelus Organ Co. in 1927, the instrument is played by Browne's descendants today. Oak pews line the length of the room.

RIGHT: Intellectuals from the Arroyo community and professors from Browne's beloved Occidental College often gathered in what is still called the "chapel" of his abbey. The vaulted ceilings are supported by recycled redwood beams Browne found at the sites of old bridges. The printer rescued the stained-glass windows from the bar of the old Van Nuys Hotel when it was dismantled during prohibition. Like the windows, the lighting fixture is made from colorful glass from Judson Studios. Above the fireplace is the chapel's requisite choir loft. LEFT: Browne designed the round window as a tribute to his printing craft, and the tiny segments' individual color codes are still on file at the glass studio should any piece need to be replaced. Browne pounded the copper sheathing on the corner fireplace and emblazoned it with his huge monogram.

CASA PEQUEÑA

Tomas Braverman, a native Angeleno, was enchanted by Mexican ecclesiastical architecture all his life. It was the Convento Carmen in Mexico City that provided inspiration for his Casa Pequeña. Everything about the house he designed, from its prominent apselike front wing to the church artifacts displayed throughout, reflects his fascination with things spiritual. Yet, he says, the house is not one pure style but rather a reverent amalgam of Hispanic, Moorish, American Southwestern, and Mediterranean cultures.

A master wood carver by profession, Braverman built the house with his own hands, lovingly crafting each detail, including the Spanish Baroque front door, the cabinetry throughout the residence, much of its furniture, and even the massive wood gates that open onto the cobbled entry courtyard. His workshop is attached to the southeast corner of the house, and it is here that he creates one-of-a-kind furniture, gates, and doors, all with a timeless quality reminiscent of the Spanish Colonial antiques that inspire him.

For the site of his house, Braverman selected a rustic undeveloped area of the city, Topanga Canyon, and placed the house in a shady oak grove. Chickens and geese play in the yard, while ducks waddle to a tiny nearby creek. It looks as if the house has been on this serene hillside for centuries; few would believe its first stones were laid in 1969.

Even with this awe-inspiring locale, most first-time visitors to the house are unprepared for the spectacular vision that greets them once inside the front door. There Braverman has dedicated the entire ground floor to a softly lit gallery containing his treasured *santos* and angel statues. The celestial mood was Braverman's goal—it is a home where troubles are left behind.

LEFT: Seen through the front door is the gallery, where a *trastero*, or cupboard, Braverman built is the only functional piece of furniture. The rest of the room is devoted to spiritual artifacts and paintings. The terracotta tiles in the floor are laid on the diagonal, which is typical of old Mexican churches. A band of blue and white floor tiles frames the room.

RIGHT: Braverman recalled the cobblestones in colonial Mexican towns when he set about placing each stone in the motor court of Casa Pequeña. Today, chickens pecking grain meander around the house. Inside the apse is Braverman's business office. To its left, behind the Moorish-inspired gates, is the yard where the craftsman stores his precious new woods and the finished works before they are shipped to their final destinations.

RIGHT: The Spanish Baroque motif painted above the windows complements the delicately detailed mullions and frames Braverman designed for his family homestead. The weathered wooden chair looks as if it has been in its position for centuries.

LEFT: Kiyo Braverman's rendering of a Mexican colonial mythological design embellishes the floor-to-ceiling fireplace. The coffee table is made from a small polished oak door. On top of it stands a wooden *santa*, a female saint figure, from Spain. On the wall above the Mexican colonial chest is a collection of *retablos* and iron *aldabas*, or latches and hasps, some of which date back four centuries.
ABOVE: Braverman's favorite Spanish Baroque motifs appear on a shower door in the bathroom.

LEFT: In a tiny vestibule off the downstairs gallery, a tapestry hangs next to an original Baroque door from a Spanish convent. The small carved chest is Mexican colonial. In the foreground, under the seventeenth-century oil painting, are an intricately carved wooden chest and corbels that were once parts of an altar in a Portuguese church. ABOVE: Directly adjoining the living room is the kitchen. Lit by a Mexican Baroque chandelier, the Portuguese tiles on the counter glisten. Another old oak door forms the surface of the dining table. Braverman carved the *trastero* that augments the Mexican cabinetry.

GIBSON / OLIVAS HOUSE

ABOVE: Mexican folk artists have come up with inventive ways to weave mundane occurrences into their Day of the Dead ceramic pieces. In this miniature scene, skeletons play billiards with a set of skulls.

Native Angelenos Christopher Gibson and Arturo Olivas both spend their lives devoted to spiritual pursuits. Gibson is a noted astrologer and teacher, and Olivas is a *retablo* artist who paints the images of saints on tin or wooden plaques.

Every room of the apartment reflects their deep involvement with both traditional religions and the mystical—with a decidedly L.A. twist. In one room, a shrine outlined in neon houses Christian symbols from Peru. In a hallway, "the household altar to the Virgin," as they call it, is strung with amusing Christmas lights. It's a colorful feast for the eyes, yet the overall feeling is reverent. Many of the religious objects are from Mexico, including *retablos*, ornamental candlesticks, angels, and clay Day of the Dead skeleton figures that are used in the Mexican folk celebration of All Souls' Day. "We have tried to achieve a spirit of joy and peace here, so that whoever visits feels better as soon as he walks in," says Gibson.

Furnishings are simple and few, to keep the focus on the vivid mélange of art and artifacts displayed throughout the apartment. By day, sunlight floods through this typical Spanish Colonial Revival duplex house, reflecting off its gently curved white walls to form the perfect setting. At night, Gibson and Olivas rely on candlelight to illuminate their magical rooms.

LEFT: *Retablo* artist Arturo Olivas, who shares this space with Christopher Gibson, is a descendant of the Tarahumara Indians of northern Mexico, the tribe that crafted the assortment of pots shown here on top of a bureau. This personal shrine also includes tin candlesticks and traditional Catholic imagery. BELOW: Symmetrically

arranged on the mantelpiece are *hojalata*, or tin-leaf, candlesticks from Southern Mexico, some of which are used for religious purposes. In the middle is a clay Tree of Life depiction of Adam and Eve.

LEFT: Gibson and Olivas's household altar to the virgin is an eclectic and pleasing jumble of objects with personal and religious meaning, including a multitude of rosaries, two of Olivas's own hand-painted *retablos*, and a string of Christmas lights. BELOW: A striped Mexican blanket brightens one end of a lodgepole bed, while dotting the wall at the head of the bed is a collection of crosses from Mexico and Los Angeles, as well as several by noted wood-carver Gloria Lopez, of Cordova, New Mexico. A table holds a still life containing a newly made Mexican blue mercury-glass bottle molded in the shape of Our Lady of Gaudalupe, Haitian decorative ironwork, and a wooden angel carved by Epifanio Fuentes, of Oaxaca, Mexico. RIGHT: A little divine inspiration helps make cleaning the dishes more tolerable. The Cuban black madonna above the faucet is Nuestra Señora de Regla.

BELOW: The residents have aggressively brought devotional fervor into their decor. Their decidedly L.A. neon shrine houses a *Cruz de la Pasión* from Peru, along with other mystical symbols of the crucifixion.

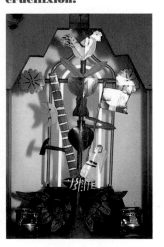

JAMES/BARTLETT HOUSE

LEFT: A studious collector of religious statuary, Peter Bartlett has displayed only a few of his favorite seraphs and saints in prominent positions in his home. The graceful madonna figure in the corner of the breakfast room was made in Mexico in the 1860s. The double doors lead to a redwood sun deck that is surrounded by fruit trees and a small patch of lawn. ABOVE: Intermingled among a rare collection of pre-Columbian pots are small wooden figures from colonial Guatemala and Mexico that Bartlett has collected on frequent buying trips south of the border. Most of the *santos* and Roman soldiers displayed are from the nineteenth century, but the *animas* statues on the lower shelf are from the eighteenth-century colonial period. They represent re-penting sinners trying to emerge from purgatory, their plight symbolized by the red flames engulfing their lower bodies. BELOW: Rather than remodel

and expand their small bungalow, as many contemporary Angelenos have, Bartlett and his wife, Claudia James, have chosen to preserve its late-Craftsman flavor and intimate ambiance. The Greek Revival porch with its paired columns is original to the structure. Columns were occasionally employed to glamorize otherwise modest bungalows.

This small 1917 Craftsman-style bungalow, with its humble Greek Revival façade, fits in harmoniously on a city block that has remarkably intact old bungalows lined up shoulder to shoulder—so many, in fact, that this area in the flatlands of Hollywood is frequently used by film crews to evoke early Los Angeles. But the neighborhood and the house's plain exterior give no clue to its contents.

The owners are Claudia James, who works in advertising, and her husband, Peter Bartlett, an art and antiques dealer. The couple has an eclectic collection of family-owned early American and English furniture, Native American rugs, and a dazzling array of nineteenth-century carved wood angels and saints, both large and small, which gaze out compellingly from every room, including the bathroom. Most of these figures are found by Bartlett on his frequent trips to Guatemala and Mexico, and they have gradually replaced the couple's contemporary art pieces.

The feeling of this home is far from pious, despite the fact that it is filled with church objects. It is spirited, not spiritual; livable, not sacrosanct. "I like being surrounded by what I think are poetic and beautiful things—it's their beauty that appeals to me," explains Bartlett. "They were objects of veneration and worship, and they were made with conviction. Unlike contemporary art, each of these objects once served a purpose, and I find that satisfying."

LEFT: Decorating the mantel in the living room are miniature topiary trees, a pair of Mexican tin candelabra from the 1940s, and a Mexican wood carving of a *doloroso*, a sorrowful figure representing a saint who prays for Christ at one of the fourteen stations of the cross in the Holy Land. Reflecting the saint is an Arts and Crafts–style mirror, the frame of which was made in Los Angeles in the 1920s. In the foreground, on the Pennsylvania oak bench, is a pair of turn-of-the-century tin altar candleholders from Mexico. LEFT: On the antique American chest of drawers in their bedroom, James and Bartlett have placed a treasure trove of Mexican collectibles, including tin candlesticks, a small nineteenth-century carving of a saint, and a glass vase from the 1940s. The image in the mirror, which is framed in ornate hammered and cut tin, is a Guatemalan *santo* that stands next to the bed.

LEFT: An American Indian rug from the 1920s adds texture to the mix of woods in the dining room. On the table are a pair of Filipino church figures dating back to 1875. The dining room is in the middle of the small house and has an attached sunroom, which provides access to the outdoors. ABOVE: A collection of Mexican *retablos*, circa 1830, surrounds an octagonal painting of the madonna and child from the nineteenth century. The English farm table, which holds New Mexican iron candlesticks with Guatemalan funeral candles, blends perfectly with the West Virginia plantation chairs and the Egyptian Revival lamp from the 1920s. The American bowl on the floor is filled with drinking gourds.

LEFT: An early landscape of Los Angeles and its majestic palm trees hangs above a grouping of small statuary. The largest figure is a nineteenth-century articulated angel from Guatemala, typical of those used in Easter parades.

LEFT: In the living-room area of artist Michael Hackett's loft, a magnificent eighteenth-century Dutch wood angel gestures on a table, while a tiger in a Victorian painting looms in the mirror's reflection. ABOVE: A sleigh bed designed by Los Angeles artist Tony Mack is draped with a star-motif silk cover and provides a dramatic sleeping area in one corner of the loft. At one edge of the marblelike walls, a broken angel appears to struggle to break free. Hackett's bedside shrine is dominated by a mixed-media "Barbie Infanta" by Los Angeles artist Sabato Fiorello. Also on display are more traditional religious symbols, including a collection of madonna figurines and Buddhas. The photograph is by Berry Berenson. RIGHT: A quirky reliquary, holding a headless composite angel wearing a chain belt, hangs precariously above a doorway.

There's no denying the ethereal quality of this unusual industrial loft space in West Hollywood, a neighborhod that is home to a plethora of the city's most creative people. "I always wanted my house to be a little bit like a temple," says artist Michael Hackett. Hackett lives with, at last count, sixty angels and cupids, all scattered throughout his home. They turn up in the most unpredictable places—a foot here, a pair of wings there. When Hackett once jokingly halved an old wooden Italian *putto* and hung up its torso to get a laugh out of a friend, the angel looked as if it had just flown through the wall. He found the effect mesmerizing and playful. Hackett is more interested in the symbolism of angels than in any traditional religious connotation.

Angels float on his walls, rest on table-tops, and even secure light switches. Hackett has collected most of them on his travels through France, Italy, and Mexico. The heavenly aura of his space is enhanced by his own "fantasy finish," neither marble  nor granite but rather a painted effect that gives objects the appearance of having aged gracefully. His ceilings are painted with the moon and stars, and collections of crystals and glass add to the otherworldly mood of his environment.

LEFT: Hackett has left no corner untouched by his heavenly inspiration, including this kitchen light switch. **RIGHT:** In the main entrance, the bottom of an Italian angel protrudes from a wall while the cherub's hand clutches yet another light switch.

ABOVE: Hackett painted the ceiling of his hallway with the moon and stars. A partially eclipsed terra-cotta angel holds a piece of crystal and hovers overhead. **RIGHT:** Elegant antique furnishings fill the expansive loft and provide an ironic contrast to its corrugated metal ceiling. The kneeling angel in the distant blue window is from the Philippines, while an Italian angel rests on a seashell table in the foreground. On a side table at right, Hackett constructed a decorative neoclassical sculpture from an iron church stand, a magnifying glass, and a crystal ball.

LEFT: Hackett's passion for flowers matches his feelings for angels. In the kitchen, a lattice-covered wall is festooned with bunches of dried roses, each one of which Hackett has romantically recycled from a fresh bouquet. A profusion of seasonal fresh flowers is always displayed in unexpected spots throughout the loft. RIGHT: Kitchen shelves display over-sized angel plates from Lisbon.

LEFT: Visitors to the loft never know where an angel will surface next. Here, the fanciful imagery extends to a kitchen counter, where a cheese grater holds a surprise. BELOW: A bear that has sprouted mystical wings serves a useful role as a razor stand in the bathroom.

KING/KNOP HOUSE

A bevy of larger-than-life angel and saint figures are silhouetted against glowing stained-glass windows to create a wonderland in this expressive house.

Patricia Louisiana Knop sees the religious figures she collects as a "connective rod between earth and something

higher." The statues of saints and angels stand at every turn inside the Mediterranean-style house where she and her husband, film director Zalman King, retreat into a joyous and colorful world.

Knop, a screenwriter and sculptor, says the couple's collection is based not on any traditional religious belief but rather on the "concept of joy. I only pick figures whose faces border on ecstasy."

The house, which, ironically, was once a 1920s speakeasy, is now filled with choice turn-of-the-century stained-glass windows, many rescued from demolished churches, as well as with Knop's own huge ceramic sculptures.

In what was originally the ballroom and is now a family gathering place, furniture is secondary to the menagerie of carousel animals poised dramatically alongside a collection of Knop's sculptures and favorite angels.

An otherworldly sense of awe overcomes visitors from the moment they enter the large gate that shields the house from the street. Even the garden, with its tangled mass of exotic flora and almost-hidden pieces of sculpture, continues the enchanted mood of this very private sanctuary.

RIGHT: Natural light floods through the windows surrounding three carved wood *santos*. Knop says she has collected holy figures all over the world, but most, like these, are from Mexico. For her, being surrounded by the figures, even in the TV room, where these stand, "imparts a sense of joy and well-being." FAR RIGHT: Joy and well-being are indeed the pervasive mood in the living room. "Most of our angels are looking upward," Knop says, referring especially to the nineteenth-century wooden angel from Mexico whose wings span the tiled coffee table. In the background is a Tiffany stained-glass window that was about to be thrown away when a Greene and Greene house in Pasadena was demolished. The art deco banister is assembled from pieces salvaged from the ticket booth of the old Redondo Beach Fox Theater.

LEFT: In a quiet corner, the owners combine a Craftsman lamp with a stained-glass shade, an elaborate table decorated with Victorian tiles, an Art Nouveau chair rescued from a Michigan barn, and this trio of Guatemalan archangels, circa 1700, that the couple found in Santa Fe, New Mexico. RIGHT: This angel, whose wings hug the sofa, was once the figurehead on a ship in the 1800s. The window behind it is from a cathedral in Buffalo, New York, and was designed by the Mayer company of Munich. Overseeing the room is Knop's sculpture of her parents and, to the right, her three-dimensional portrait of daughter Gillian as a lion. The snow leopard once rode on a nineteenth-century carousel.

LEFT: The ballroom features a collection of carousel animals, such as the horse seen here, which originally belonged to a carousel in Los Angeles's Luna Park in the 1880s. When some Hollywood filmmakers saw this Mexican angel, circa 1815, they duplicated it and used the reproduction in the 1990 film *Ghost*. The miniature church is Early American folk art, and the turn-of-the-century art-glass window is by Tiffany. ABOVE: The velvet sofa is a refurbished Chinese opium couch that is thought to have belonged to silent-screen star Mary Astor. At the right, an altar angel saved from an old American church has been wired as a lamp. On the wall, a section of a collapsible tent used for country boxing matches in England makes an unusual backdrop for the otherwise ethereal decor. On the angel table, an Ecuadoran wood sculpture depicts Christ forgiving the sins of a mortal.

FLETCHER HOUSE

LEFT: Seen from the east, facing the pyramid home of Bill and Sally Fletcher, are the magnificent Santa Monica Mountains, sheathed in natural mountain chaparral, scrub oak, and toyon, or California holly. Although the hills are green year 'round, in the winter, when this photograph was taken, the landscape is even more vibrant. Six varieties of palm trees as well as acacia trees grow near the house. At the right, a row of Italian cypress trees line a path leading to the or-

chard. ABOVE: A fifties-style molded plastic chair is poised in the living room. It is placed in front of the pyramid's west wall, which offers the finest view, and, therefore, is almost entirely made of glass. RIGHT: The Fletchers plan to cover the walls of their as-yet-unfinished living room and entry hall with wood and stone.
ABOVE, FAR RIGHT: The

east wall has a single protruding octagonal window. The eight-sided shape reappears on the windows of the pyramid's two wings, which house a library and a den. Both wings are decagon-shaped and have vertical walls, a form initially chosen not only for its artistic merit but also for psychological reasons. After living most of their lives in traditional structures, the Fletchers anticipated that there would be times when they might need relief from being in a house with slanted walls.

One of the most spectacular sights in all Los Angeles County is to be found where the Santa Monica Mountains meet the Pacific Ocean, in Malibu. Equally astounding is to travel the winding road that leads from that beach into a nearby canyon and to happen upon the dream house that Bill and Sally Fletcher built—a pyramid modeled after the Great Pyramid in Egypt.

To the Fletchers, who are astronomers and astrophotographers, the historical and metaphysical references of their house's shape were key. "A pyramid is a pure form, so living inside one becomes like living inside an archetypal symbol. It supports and reinforces the artist in you," says Bill Fletcher. Here, the Fletchers can look out their window both day and night and see the sun, the stars, and the moon and be reminded of their place on this planet.

Although not an ordinary house by any means, their pyramid is surprisingly traditional. There's a study and a den, a kitchen with all the modern conveniences, even a piano in the living room. Sally grows her own fruits and vegetables in a sizable orchard on their 2½-acre site. A spiral stairway leads to the master bedroom, the only room that hovers close to the structure's apex, the spatial equivalent of the King's Chamber area of the Great Pyramid. There, a huge expanse of glass allows the Fletchers to wake and retire with the heavens in view.

7

Los Angeles is the ultimate city on wheels. Other metropolises are defined by their skylines; L.A. is **Impact of the Automobile** defined by its freeways. The automobile has shaped the cityscape since the turn of the century, determining the spread of the suburbs, the architecture of commercial structures and houses, and, in some cases, interior design.

LEFT: When Bullock's Wilshire department store opened on September 26, 1929, its design, by architects John and Donald B. Parkinson, reflected the automobile revolution that was overtaking Los Angeles. It was the first of the city's major department stores to have two entrances, one on Wilshire Boulevard and another, the primary one, beneath a porte cochere at the back of the building, facing the parking lot. On the ceiling of the porte cochere is a hand-painted mural depicting the history of transportation. At the entrances to the drive are Art Deco iron gates representing the theme "Time Flies." In 1988, the store merged with another prestigious retailer and was renamed I. Magnin Bullocks Wilshire, the Landmark Store. BELOW: Angelenos are known to turn their cars into personal statements, such as the expressively decorated vehicle parked here. ABOVE: The coach house of an estate designed by Bertram Goodhue in 1917 has been modernized into a contemporary home. Goodhue probably never considered displaying a car in the living room, but that's exactly what owners Janet and Tim Walker have done with their 1956 Siata 208S Spider. A 1937 Indian Four motorcycle stands in the background.

The car has influenced the ways Angelenos shop, eat, work, play, and even make love. People here idolize cars and extol their virtues in song, on celluloid, and on canvas. It could be argued that no city, not even Detroit, is more culturally and emotionally attached to the car than L.A.

More than just a mode of transportation, the auto is a symbol of freedom and mobility, the only way to experience the sprawling county—fully 4000 square miles. With deserts, mountains, and beaches all within an hour's drive and weather that's conducive to driving year-round, the car is more than a functional necessity—it is an escape vehicle. Driving is an easy way to flee the pressures of home, the workplace, or civilization entirely. So just about every Angeleno of driving age finds a way to put his or her foot to the gas pedal.

Statistics speak for themselves. Approximately 5.5 million of the nearly 9 million residents of greater Los Angeles are licensed drivers, steering 4.6 million cars. Add to that 1.4 million motorcycles, buses, and trucks, for a total of 6 million L.A. vehicles on the road. Consequently, the 500 miles of freeways that lace through the area are the busiest in the world.

A century ago, the car had just made its debut on Los Angeles streets, and few people then could possibly anticipate what it would mean to the city or the way its people would live. Even finding space to house a car was a novel idea. If a garage existed on an individual's property, it was most probably a carriage house or small stable for horses, buggies, and bicycles, the main modes of personal transportation at the time. A few Craftsman bungalows had enclosed spaces for cars, but the concept was new and unusual. The Automobile Club of Southern California was founded in 1900, but catered to hobbyists who made a sport of motoring.

At that time, the primary mode of pub-

BELOW RIGHT: The allure of the automobile swelled as movieland dream makers appealed to the fantasies of wartime Americans. In the same way that costume designers draped female stars in satins and furs, set designers and clever public-relations executives outfitted male stars with expensive, sexy cars, like the jaunty roadster actor Franchot Tone posed with here. **BELOW:** Though remembered as one of Southern California's most important businessmen, railroad magnate and real estate tycoon Henry E. Huntington didn't move his business operations to Los Angeles until he was fifty-two, and by age sixty he had retired. But in those few years he developed the existing railroad system into one of the most extensive interurban systems in the West. Because of his shrewd and extremely profitable railroad and real estate moves, the region experienced dramatic population growth. After he retired to devote his attention to his fine-art, rare-book, and manuscript collections, he married Arabella Duval Huntington, the widow of his uncle Collis, the man who had introduced him to railroads. Together they developed the collections that are the basis of today's library and galleries.

lic mass transit was the streetcar. In 1873, horse-drawn cars began operating—the area's first transportation innovation since 1869, when Phineas Banning developed the port at Wilmington, near Long Beach, and linked the harbor to downtown Los Angeles via a small railroad. (That small strip of railroad track would eventually lure the Southern Pacific to route its line through the city.) These streetcars, which were electrified in 1887, enabled people to move to the outskirts of town without a daunting commute.

In the heart of downtown, at the southwest corner of Third and Hill streets, a unique cable car called Angel's Flight was built in 1901 and would remain one of the city's favorite tourist attractions until it was removed in 1969. Often billed as the world's shortest passenger railway, its 350 feet of track climbed Bunker Hill to a vista point dubbed Angel's Rest, where visitors could view the city for a nickel. The funicular and its station house were taken out of storage and restored in 1991, and eventually two orange-and-black cars, named Olivet and Sinai, will be returned to service.

By 1895, a network of small interurban railways had developed in outlying areas. Like the streetcar-line owners, the railway entrepreneurs were also clever real estate developers who built the lines to access regions where they had bought great expanses of undeveloped, inexpensive land. With convenient transportation as a lure, these speculators sold thousands of plots in outlying areas at prices that were within the reach of many people's pocketbooks, especially those Midwesterners who had followed Horace Greeley's advice and flocked to the West. As more and more people bought property in areas as distant as Santa Monica to the west, San Bernardino in the east, the San Fernando Valley in the north, and Long Beach to the south, the rail network determined the primary arteries of travel and the urban sprawl that define the city today.

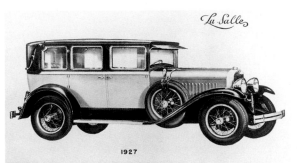
La Salle
1927

Entrepreneur Henry E. Huntington, the nephew of Central Pacific Railroad co-founder Collis P. Huntington, quickly recognized the power and money to be gained from controlling public transportation in a city like Los Angeles. Through a series of mergers and acquisitions around the turn of the century, Huntington consolidated the dozens of existing small interurban lines to form the Pacific Electric Railway, or the famous Big Red Cars. This network of standard-gauge railways operated along with his smaller streetcar system, the Los Angeles Electric. So overwhelming was his monopoly and resulting fortune that Huntington became one of the richest men in America. His lavish estate, with its Beaux-Arts neoclassic mansion designed by Myron Hunt and Elmer Grey in 1910, is known today as the Huntington Library, Art Collections, and Botanical Gardens. The collection includes a Gutenberg Bible, Thomas Gainsborough's *Blue Boy*, Sir Thomas Lawrence's *Pinkie*, the manuscript for Thoreau's *Walden*, and an extensive collection of Shakespeare.

By 1910, Huntington's railway system covered 377 miles of the city and eventually blanketed the area with more than 1000 miles of track. But the Pacific Electric's undeniable success was also its downfall. The mul-

ABOVE: The original 1927 LaSalle—the most luxurious American car of its era—was designed by Angeleno Harley Earl, who went on to redesign the Cadillac and eventually become a vice-president of General Motors. Designing cars was in his blood; his father had owned Earl Carriage Works in Los Angeles. RIGHT: This 1936 Ford roadster is but one of a vast collection of vintage cars owned by film industry auto consultant Tom Sparks (see page 213). BELOW: Call it a conceptual art piece on wheels or simply a crazy custom auto—this pickup is festooned with decals, bumper stickers, and an assortment of toys and treasures.

titude of trains resulted in Los Angeles's first dose of twentieth-century congestion. By 1920, to serve a population of more than a half million people (the city's population had increased fivefold since the turn of the century and would surpass the million mark by 1930), the Pacific Electric system had become too big, with too many intersections—the results were frequent accidents, botched schedules, major slowdowns, and disappointed commuters. Suddenly, the company was faced with the reality that Angelenos were taking transportation into their own hands: they were buying cars and were no longer depending on the rails. More than 150,000 cars were registered in 1920, and by 1940 there would be one million.

Glamorous movie stars also helped spread the notion of L.A. as Car Town. In old Hollywood and Beverly Hills, expensive cars carried as much status as the huge mansions the stars lived in. At chic restaurants and film premieres, screen sirens in satin dresses and feathered boas emerged from the back of chauffeur-driven automobiles as the cameras flashed. And part of the sex appeal of male stars was directly linked to the kinds of jaunty new roadsters in which they were photographed for studio publicity stills.

The American public frequently equated what they saw on the silver screen with what real life was like in Los Angeles. So sporty convertibles and luxurious town cars, the kind that filmmakers loved to include in everything from the earliest Keystone Kops chase scenes to the present-day James Bond wonder-wagon battles, became part of the idealized image of the city—an image the rest of the country wanted to emulate.

Detroit auto manufacturers began to value popular opinion in Los Angeles because they had quickly learned that Southern California trends influenced the country's buying patterns. If a new model scored in L.A., chances were good it would be a hit elsewhere too. Detroit began importing car designers from Los Angeles—in fact, General Motors' 1927 LaSalle was designed by L.A. native Harley Earl, who went on to supervise design for the firm until the late fifties. The tradition continues: today, the Art Center College of Design in Pasadena boasts one of the world's most important industrial design departments. In addition, nearly every major auto producer has an advanced design studio strategically located in the Southern California area. Los Angeles was also once the nation's second largest auto-making center, behind Detroit, but that era ended in August 1992, when General Motors closed the area's last remaining auto assembly plant, built in 1947 in Van Nuys. Since 1970, car makers had been moving to lower-wage factories abroad or in other U.S. regions.

By 1930, Los Angeles was showing the architectural signs of being a town on the roll. More drive-in establishments dotted the landscape than in any other city. Drive-in restaurants, markets, shopping centers, and auto repair shops were popping up all over. Tourists who drove to L.A. probably stayed in one of the hundreds of newfangled motels at roadsides. (The term, combining "motor" and "hotel," was concocted by inventor Alfred Heineman for the Milestone Motel that his brother Arthur designed in

San Luis Obispo, a few hours north of Los Angeles.) Businessmen, in hopes of distinguishing their buildings from others, perched tall towers—which couldn't be missed from the road—atop their establishments. Posh department stores, such as Bullock's Wilshire (1929) and, later, the May Company (1940), placed main entrances under fancy porte-cocheres that faced their parking lots, not the street. And other shopping strips, like the Miracle Mile near La Brea Tar Pits, developed parking access at the rear rather than frontal pedestrian entrances. (The trend hasn't changed in sixty years. Today a grand row of Wilshire Boulevard department stores in Beverly Hills still features main entries at the rear, with doormen and valets who escort shoppers to their cars.)

In the mid-thirties, residents of Pasadena, South Pasadena, and Los Angeles joined forces with the state to fund the building of a 6-mile stretch of roadway to shorten the driving time from downtown to Pasadena. It opened in 1940 at a cost of $5.7 million. Filled with death-defying on-ramps and off-ramps, this curving stretch of the city's historic transportation system is still a major artery into and out of downtown. And although there were freeways in other parts of the country first—in Detroit and New York, for example—the Arroyo Seco Parkway, part of what is known as the Pasadena Freeway today, was the first segment of L.A.'s famous roadway network. But it wasn't until after World War II that construction began on the rest of the freeways. As the system expanded, its routes made the door-to-door convenience of driving a luxury most people were determined to afford.

Since almost every family had a car, a place to store it became as vital to a home as indoor plumbing. Year-round moderate weather meant that a garage need not be enclosed to protect an automobile. But prolonged exposure to the sun could ruin a car's exterior. Thus the carport, a roof extending from a building to cover the car, became an ingenious low-cost solution used by both Modernists and traditionalists. Real estate developers also copied the concept in low-cost housing tracts. The owners of big estates in the exclusive neighborhoods of Beverly Hills, Hancock Park, and Pasadena converted carriage houses into garages, often with room for several cars. Grand circular drives or miniature brick roads that wound their way up to hillside estates became symbols of success; the richest folk had drivers and guards who worked in their gate houses.

After World War II, as the spokes of the freeway system spread to the affordable suburbs, the style of houses began to change. On larger lots, houses could sprawl. The low, rambling, urban ranch house was the ideal California dream house. The single-story style combined several historical references to the state's past—a touch of Craftsman bungalow; a bit of Mission, with courtyards, patios, and long wings; even a smattering of nineteenth-century California farmhouse, with board-and-batten siding covering the exteriors. Sixth-generation Californian Cliff May is often referred to as the father of the twentieth-century ranch house. Though not an architect by training, he designed one thousand buildings across the country, including both cookie-cutter houses in middle-class tracts and expensive luxury models. By the fifties, May's designs had become totally modern, with glass sliding doors and informal room arrangements that suited the relaxed lifestyle of post–World War II Southern California. And of course he included a garage, with room for two cars. As the ranch house matured, the attached garage that led directly into the kitchen or family room became the preferred design. In the late forties and fifties,

BELOW: At the top of the winding drive that leads to the Van Pelt estate in the Los Feliz district, spiraling clinker brick lampposts mark the entrance to the motor courtyard. Architect John Van Pelt built five houses on the extensive property from 1937 to 1942. The main house, modeled after a Bavarian hunting lodge, was Van Pelt's and was perched atop a carport designed to hold several vehicles. A onetime lyric tenor, Van Pelt named the lane that leads to his estate "Lyric." BELOW RIGHT: Colorful garage doors are as much a part of the Los Angeles landscape as bougainvillea and birds of paradise. A garage is hidden behind the triple red-and-white panels on the front of this Chinatown home. BELOW: The zigs and zags of this orange-and-red garage turn the door into a vibrant and whimsical statement on an otherwise quiet street overlooking the Pacific Ocean. It was designed by Delia Heilig.

the garage often was positioned at the front of the house, creating a sound barrier from the street and establishing an acceptable new—and distinctly "L.A."—form of curb appeal that soon spread across the country.

From the fifties on, Angelenos became so attached to their cars that they hated to get out. The drive-in concept expanded to include drive-in churches, banks, fast-food restaurants, and cleaners, and by the 1980s there were psychologists who would ride in the car with patients to help cure freeway phobias. The remote-control garage door opener enabled motorists virtually to drive into their own homes without even stopping to pull out a key.

Such was the impact of the auto on L.A. Today the same factors that derailed the Pacific Electric trains—congestion, accidents, slow travel time—coupled with noise and air pollution are causing Angelenos to rethink their personal transportation habits. But even as the new 300-mile, $140-billion Metro Rail transit system is being constructed, it's clear that getting the people of Los Angeles to give up cars will be difficult at best. They're part of the culture.

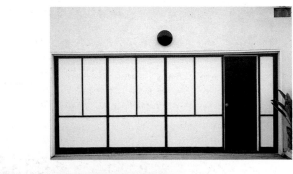

CLEWORTH HOUSE

LEFT: Cleworth designed this built-in bookshelf, crowned with a vinyl-rimmed clock, automobile paraphernalia, including a pair of 1959 Cadillac taillights, a chrome logo from a 1958 Chrysler Imperial, and toy cars. The outmoded, and nonfunctioning, turquoise dial phone has its own charm.

LEFT: A Naugahyde booth recreates the mood of a 1950s diner in a corner of Harold Cleworth's auto-theme dining room. Flowers cut from the garden spill from a recycled motor-oil can. The artwork depicting hubcaps from a 1957 Mercury and a 1957 Ford Thunderbird are Cleworth's prototypes for a series of automobile-theme china. BELOW RIGHT: A kitschy mood prevails in the dining room, with its pink-and-emerald glitter-vinyl chairs, black Formica dining table, neon-lit sideboard, wool leopard rug, and starburst chandelier. The focal point of the room is Cleworth's painting of a 1963 red Corvette Stingray. BELOW, FAR RIGHT: Above the fireplace in the living room is a Cleworth portrait of a black 1957 Chevrolet Bel Air convertible, a vehicle the artist considers the ultimate fifties driving machine. Beneath it on the mantel is a traffic jam of toy cars dated from the 1950s to the present. Cleworth also designed the kidney-shaped Formica coffee table in keeping with his favorite era.

Harold Cleworth fell in love with cars as a child growing up in industrial Northern England, but once he moved to Los Angeles, in 1974, he turned his fascination into an art form. "The first thing that hit me in the face here was the automobile. I always wanted to be a painter, so the two came together perfectly," says Cleworth, who is a noted automobile artist. Serious car collectors turn to him for portraits of their most prized possessions.

Not surprisingly, his home is a playful world of cars, car parts, and memorabilia—a world where hubcaps are transformed into tabletops and rear-view mirrors become wall sconces. Since his favorite cars were designed in the 1950s, Cleworth has also gravitated to all manner of fifties furniture and kitsch. "Everything designed in the fifties has a sense of delight about it that appeals to me," he notes.

Visitors to his 1930s bungalow in Hollywood can't help but share the delight. His striking photorealist car paintings line the wall, and his automotive *objets* appear at every turn. And on the easel in his at-home studio there's always a car-in-progress.

SPARKS HOUSE

Few people can match the period of their car to the period of their home. But seeing one of Tom Sparks's 1930s Fords parked in the driveway of this 1930s Spanish Colonial Revival house is like walking into the pages of a Raymond Chandler novel.

Sparks was raised in an Iowa farm town, moved to Los Angeles as a child in the thirties, and was dazzled by the flashy cars he saw in Hollywood. His first job was in a Packard dealership, and he never left the car world. A one-time race-car driver, he now owns an automobile restoration and repair business and, as a sideline, works as a technical adviser on movies that feature period autos.

Not surprisingly, cars have taken over his home. His collection of American cars from the twenties to the fifties fills two enormous backyard garages festooned with vintage car-related signs, emblems, hood ornaments, and miniatures. Other automobile paraphernalia is strategically placed in his backyard, including an old gas station sign and an early gasoline pump.

LEFT: One of Sparks's two garages is a virtual museum of cars and car-related embellishments. Here, a metal stone guard of the type that protected the radiators of 1920s and 1930s automobiles displays a collection of old car emblems. Behind them are pre–World War II toy cars.

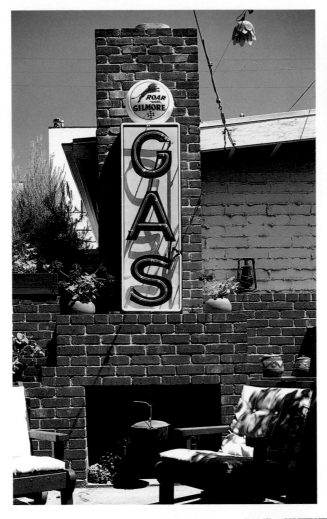

LEFT: Unabashed love of the automobile is evident all around the Sparks house and even extends into the backyard. On the patio, a working neon sign, circa 1940, taken from an abandoned gas station in Hollywood, lends a quaintly nostalgic touch to a cozy barbecue pit. The sign lights up when the family gathers round for a celebration. ABOVE: Unusual chrome-plated "mascots," or hood ornaments, from the 1920s and 1930s can be admired as sculpture. BELOW: Even in a car-driven city like L.A., gas pumps rarely figure into the domestic scene. Rarer still is this big red pre–World War II "visible gas pump," which is an eye-catching addition to the garden.

ABOVE: Suspended overhead in one of the garages is a display of gas station and oil company signs from the twenties through the fifties. In the back is one of the fiberglass engine models Sparks designed to appear on assembly lines in the 1988 movie *Tucker.*

MEYER GARAGE

CENTER LEFT: Just beneath the basketball hoop and inside the garage door is the Agajanian Special, one of Meyer's most prized autos, as it was the winning car at the 1952 Indianapolis 500. As any car enthusiast will recall, the Agajanian was driven by Troy Ruttman, the youngest winner in Indy history. The motorcycle next to it is one of eight cycles in Meyer's collection. ABOVE, NEAR LEFT: The lemon-yellow 1967 Ferrari 275 GTB4 carries a California vanity license plate with a tasty message. The garage art includes Alexander Calder prints and vivid car posters, all strategically coordinated to the colors of the cars parked nearby.

Seen from the driveway, it looks like any ordinary two-car garage equipped with the obligatory basketball hoop. But retailer Bruce Meyer, who collects "anything on wheels," built instead a superdeluxe, high-security fourteen-car garage with room to spare (there are also eight motorcycles and two bicycles).

Tucked between the 1920s English Tudor house and its modern swimming pool, this unlikely museum-type space provides parking for race cars, sports cars, and a few classics. Suitable car art is hung on the walls, including one of pop artist Mel Ramos's famed spark-plug images. The owner, a third-generation Angeleno who says he fell in love with cars "at birth," admits that his spectacular garage is a dream come true.

Meyer grew up in the fifties, listening to Chuck Berry and idolizing James Dean. In fact, his first set of wheels was a 1950 black Mercury like the one the actor drove in *Rebel Without a Cause*. Meyer's Merc is still parked in his garage, along with Clark Gable's 1955 300 S Mercedes and Dolores Del Rio's Duesenberg.

LEFT: Car aficionado Bruce Meyer's garage is really two large rooms of uninterrupted parking. In this wing, a gas pump from a Los Angeles Gilmore station occupies a central position. To the left is a snazzy black 1957 fuel-injected Corvette, and seemingly peering into it is an apropos cutout of fifties screen idol and hot rodder James Dean. This eclectic automobile collection also includes, on the right, a red 1932 Ford. ABOVE: The Corvette boasts a splashy red interior.

HULL HOUSE

Jim Hull is a man who knows how to enjoy his toys. Hull and his wife, Penny, built an additional room onto their 1921 Craftsman bungalow for the sole purpose of accommodating a hydraulic lift just like the ones found in car repair shops.

Jim, a serious car collector and founder of H.U.D.D.L.E. Furniture For Kids, wanted to be able to admire his cars in the comfort of his own living room. So he opens wide doors that lead from the garden driveway to the living room and then drives a car onto the chromed lift. A car raised two to four feet off the ground is at the "proper view level," says Jim. "I want to see my 'rolling sculptures' at the same level as the artists who designed them."

The large living space, with its dramatic twenty-two-foot-high beamed ceiling, also has room to park two cars in addition to the one on the lift. The ever-changing display may include a "H.U.D.D.L.E.-green" 1948 Delahaye and a 1965 fly-yellow Ferrari Spyder, which are painted in the same primary colors as the Hulls' furniture. The two-story river rock fireplace is adorned with car art, trophies, and antique toy sports cars.

"Driving is my sport," says Hull. In fact, since

1978, he and Penny have hosted their own Malibu-to-Brentwood Bastille Day Rally so they and their friends can celebrate driving.

ABOVE LEFT: Behind its glass doors, this deluxe car shelter is as elegant as any home. The well-tended gardens of the main house cover its roof and more lush landscaping surrounds this unusual garage. Inside, in addition to the automobiles, etched glass display cases show off this car collector's numerous trophies and prize ribbons.
LEFT: The cars on view in this palatial space are protected from glare by an intricate system of indirect lighting, which also makes their lines appear all the more sophisticated. Seen from right to left are a 1955 Mercedes-Benz 300 SL Gullwing, a 1948 Talbot Lago Record Cabriolet, a 1947 Talbot Lago Grand Sport with body designed in Paris by J. Saoutchik, a 1958 Mercedes-Benz 300 SL Roadster, and a 1972 Ferrari Daytona.

GRASS-TOPPED GARAGE

LEFT: In this luxurious underground garage, dramatically silhouetted against a beautifully landscaped drive and positioned in a place of prominence on its own turntable, is a Super-Charged 1938 Bugatti Type 57C.

There aren't too many home-owners in Los Angeles who landscape the roof of their garage with grass and trees. The businessman who built this high-toned stable for his herd of cars literally moved the earth to build a 3,500-square-foot underground automobile environment. But, then, not everyone owns thoroughbreds like a Super-Charged 1938 Bugatti Type 57C, a 1902 Darracq, or a red 1972 Ferrari Daytona.

It took two years to excavate a hole where a paddle-tennis court once stood and then build this subterranean garage at the end of a long, sloping driveway. The nouveau-Colonial space, designed by architect Kip Kelly, comes complete with pilasters and columns like those in the main house. The chamber is equipped with amenities such as a cocktail bar, a video-viewing area, a high-tech sound system, copper tubing to heat the floor, and a full-sized chrome turntable for the vehicles. The owner wants his friends to enjoy the collection too—the garage easily accommodates sit-down dinners for 150.

Kitsch, fantasy, glamour, extremism—or whatever you want to call it—pervade life at every turn in L.A. At least that's the image most outsiders pin on the city. To the rest of the world it may be La-La Land, but actually a good share of Angelenos rather relish the ribbing. L.A. is as idiosyncratic as its inhabitants, and they seem to like it that way. The fact is, unconventionality is simply intrinsic to the culture. Creative license and personal expression

Follies

LEFT: In the thirties, sightseers would take a stroll on Hollywood Boulevard just to look at the dreamy movie palaces with their fantastic marquees and peek in at their opulent interiors. What a sight it was—first the gaudy Egyptian Theater, then the incredible Chinese Theater, and then, across the street, the ornate El Capitan, with its sumptuous Indian interior by G. Albert Lansburgh, a noted theater designer from San Francisco. The magnificent Venetian Renaissance molded-plaster and gilded dome over its outer ticket lobby, seen here, was designed by Morgan, Walls & Clements, the firm responsible for the Spanish Colonial Re-

vival façade. Originally built for stage productions, El Capitan quickly became known for lavish motion-picture premieres after its first film, *Citizen Kane*, opened in 1941. BELOW: The building housing El Capitan is a six-story office complex believed to have once been a furniture company. Over the years, El Capitan changed hands and was at one time renamed the Paramount.

During various remodeling processes, Lansburgh's elaborate interiors were almost lost. But Buena Vista Pictures Distribution and Pacific Theaters restored the theater both inside and out and reopened the film palace as El Capitan in 1991. ABOVE RIGHT: The Donut Hole in La Puente is the consummate drive-through concept. It was designed in 1968 by John Tindall, Ed Mc-Creany, and Jesse Hood as a modern throwback to the programmatic architecture that blossomed in 1930s Los Angeles. Like the Tail of the Pup hot dog stand, shaped like a giant frankfurter in a bun, this "donut" is one of the city's most photographed eateries.

come with the territory. And it's apparent everywhere you look.

There is no better way to account for loopy everyday sights such as the Donut Hole (1932), the drive-through-the-hole establishment shaped like the food; the Hard Rock Cafe (1982), a restaurant conceived by owner Peter Morton with a '59 Cadillac crashing through its roof; the Samson Tyre and Rubber Company factory, dressed as an Assyrian palace (Morgan, Walls & Clements, 1929), now a discount clothing outlet; and Burbank's Walt Disney Studio headquarters (Michael Graves, 1991), where the Seven Dwarfs, with arms raised overhead, function as columns supporting a postmodern pediment.

The entire beachside town of Venice was the 1905 invention of developer Abbot Kinney, who routed bridge-covered canals through the coastal community in hopes of recreating the romantic Italian city. That was a half century before another fantasy world took shape: Disneyland opened in nearby Anaheim in 1955, showcasing in-

BELOW: The dramatic pagoda roof and a guardian dragon signal audiences and tourists that they have arrived at one of Hollywood's best-known landmarks, the Chinese Theater. Here, star-struck fans can match their hand- and footprints to those of their favorite screen stars. BELOW LEFT: Almost a century after Abbot Kinney developed his fantasy network of canals to simulate Venice, Italy, his dream lives on in Venice, California. Today, many of the tiny bungalows that once lined the canals are being replaced by large modern houses. BOTTOM: Entering the world of tomorrow at Disneyland when it opened in 1955 meant advancing to "the world of 1987." Monsanto's all-plastic "Home of the Future" was filled with ultramodern furnishings and concepts. By the mid-sixties, however, its remarkable futuristic designs were already dated and the home was permanently closed, even though the rest of Tomorrowland was completely updated.

ventive city planning at its apex. Its faux Matterhorn, faux Bavarian castle, and faux Main Street U.S.A. are linked by a futuristic monorail system. By 1966, however, the original Tomorrowland was closed because the world had caught up with Walt Disney's visionaries. It was completely redesigned and reopened the following year.

In fact, the entertainment industry provides the city not only with an important source of revenue but with its greatest source of architectural playfulness, adventure, and drama. Year-round sunshine attracted filmmakers to Los Angeles as early as 1907, when the Selig Polyscope film company made the one-reel melodrama *The Count of Monte Cristo*. In 1915, D. W. Griffith filmed the spectacle *Intolerance* on a garish, 300-foot-high Babylonian set, complete with monumental statues of goddesses and elephants. The crumbling remains of the set stood for several years at the intersection of Sunset and Hollywood boulevards, where passersby would ogle in wonder. At about the same time, Universal Pictures opened its studio lot to visitors who could watch movies being made for free. That novelty presaged the Universal Studios Tour, where sightseers pay to behold mechanized sharks, extraterrestrials, and simulated earthquakes re-created from popular movies.

As film studios cranked out movies from one end of the city to the other, theater design was also bigger than life and added to the fantasy. The flashy shrines to cinema included the aptly named Egyptian (Meyer and Holler, 1922), Chinese (Meyer and Holler, 1927), and Mayan (Morgan, Walls & Clements, 1926–27) theaters, as well as the Spanish Colonial Revival–style El Capitan (Morgan, Walls & Clements, 1926), which was completely refurbished in 1991. All were thickly encrusted with ornamentation from the appropriate culture,

a local drive-in, fanfare was half the fun. The same concept worked with architecture. Even on the front path to a modest home in an unassuming neighborhood, these Egyptian guards suggest that treasures worthy of King Tut lie beyond. BELOW: Similarly, "Muse of Music" at the entrance to the Hollywood Bowl amphitheater added to the glamour of a music-filled evening under the

ABOVE: In its day, *Intolerance* was the most expensive film ever made, full of the excesses that contributed to Hollywood's grandiose image. But perhaps its greatest excess was the massive set that towered above the corner where Hollywood and Sunset boulevards converge. Director D. W. Griffith's film studios were across the street. Today, a supermarket sits on the studio site and the Vista Theater occupies the old *Intolerance* locale. BELOW RIGHT: This adobe tepee is one of the more farfetched ways that an Angeleno has paid homage to the past. Walter P. Temple constructed this wacky tribute to Native Americans in the twenties, on the grounds where his grandfather, William Workman, had built the family home in 1842. The original 48,790-acre property, called Rancho La Puente, was granted to Workman by the Mexican government. Today, a remaining small parcel of the *rancho*, the Workman and Temple Family Homestead, is open to the public.

stars. Dedicated in the summer of 1940, the entrance fountain, once lit with colorful lights, took eighteen months to complete and cost more than $100,000. The kneeling figure on top is fifteen feet high and weighs thirty tons. "Music" and the ten-foot muses of dance and drama that occupy lower niches were sculpted by George Stanley.

interpreted à la Hollywood.

Film moguls and stars lived in their own private palaces, as fanciful as anything on the silver screen. The hills are still studded with their enormous homes, which often were the owner's cockeyed fantasies of wealth and breeding. Credit for the first glitzy star home goes to Douglas Fairbanks. In 1919, while courting Mary Pickford, Fairbanks hired a movie art director, Max Parker, to redesign a hunting lodge he purchased in Beverly Hills, adding a swimming pool edged with sand and ponds for canoeing. Even the house's name, Pickfair, had a certain panache. From 1926 to 1934,

ABOVE: Today, though Watts Towers, the home of Simon Rodia, has crumbled, the spires remain, covered in broken remnants of Rodia's life in Los Angeles. As if to make that point, scratched into a wall near the main entrance to the tangle of concrete and iron are the words "Nuestro Pueblo," which can be interpreted as "our town" or "our people." The entire display is protected by a tall fence, but Rodia's own scalloped version is visible just inside. BELOW: No one really knew or cared what Rodia had in mind when he started his mosaic concrete sculptures in 1921. When he finished, in 1954, little more was clear. Yet his Watts Towers have become a folk-art shrine to imagination and determination. BELOW RIGHT: Rodia embedded shells, glass, pottery, tiles, and other found objects into his creations, studding most surfaces. The two tallest towers are accompanied by smaller towers, creating a jungle of spiraling cones. Fountains, a sculpture of a ship, many pillars, and several arches can also be seen. ABOVE RIGHT: L.A.'s folk-art tradition continues today with a colorful hibachi made from old license plates by metal sculptor Ries Niemi (see page 241).

Wallace Neff, the architect preferred by the stars for his ability to stretch historicism into elegant new realities, redesigned and expanded Pickfair. The result was an aristocratic English Regency mansion to suit Hollywood's home-grown nobility. Singer/actress Pia Zadora and her husband, Meshulim Riklis, bought the forty-two-room landmark in 1988 for $6.6 million and razed it to build a Venetian-style mansion, although the original pool—minus sand—remains intact.

Entire portions of the city, such as Beachwood Canyon, one of Hollywood's oldest neighborhoods, are such charming architectural hodgepodges—fitted with side-by-side Hansel and Gretel cottages, medieval castles, classic Italian villas—that they look as if they belong on a studio back lot. And for good reason. Many of the homes were built by studio technicians who constructed movie sets by day. Today, George Ehling, a motion-picture studio carpenter and prop maker, continues the tradition with his Hollywood-Mediterranean chateau guarded by gargoyles plucked from a movie set (see page 229). Ehling has spent years sheathing the house with his own handmade mosaics. Ehling's verve, if not his undertaking, are reminiscent of another of the city's greatest follies, the grand Watts Towers, a garden of webbed iron and concrete spire sculptures covered in tile, broken bottles, glass, and china. Built by Italian immigrant Simon Rodia, the Towers are one of the world's great folk-art monuments. Rodia, a manual laborer, started assembling them in 1921, and his hobby became an obsession that lasted thirty-three

years, until he finally moved to Northern California.

Frequently, trained architects could take credit for historical hopscotching. In the twenties and thirties, the best of them, including Paul R. Williams, Roland E. Coate, and Gordon B. Kaufmann, could readily switch eras and continents. Before designing the Egyptian and Chinese theaters, Meyer and Holler first built refined period houses in the exclusive Hancock Park neighborhood.

Cecil B. De Mille deemed that movies were greatly responsible for L.A.'s visual melting pot. "The barrier of miles has been torn down," De Mille wrote in a 1925 architectural journal. "People everywhere are seeing on the screen within the space of a few hours the life, customs, and buildings of other humans in every part of the world. California types have been particularly fortunate in this respect because so many pictures are made here." In any case, it is arguable where the credit belongs. Even De Mille hired professional architects to design his period movie sets. And local legend has it that Walt Disney was inspired by a cluster of cozy little Norman cottages (Robert Sherwood, 1929) in Los Feliz, where several of his artists lived. The first sketches for the Seven Dwarfs' storybook cottage showed similar lines.

Beyond the movies, L.A. architects have invented their own unique flamboyant styles. In 1949, when John Lautner de-

BELOW: Architect John Van Pelt had an obvious flair for the theatrical—the kind that would have impressed even Cecil B. De Mille. This Egyptian-theme swimming pool, with its hand-painted bottom depicting a god with a jaguar draped over one shoulder, was part of the compound Van Pelt built for his family in the hills of the Los Feliz area.   RIGHT:

Those Cleopatra eyes casting a watchful gaze on the poolside dining area are painted on the wall, but the statue rests in its own niche. The present owner of Van Pelt's estate, Dan Hornbeck, a former actor, was attracted to the property by its drama. Hornbeck has spent the last several years restoring the lush terraced gardens that lead to the pool.

LEFT: The mansions of Beverly Hills have always been, and continue to be, a folly in their own right. But in the golden age of the motion picture, they represented real life— Hollywood style—to film audiences around the world. Somehow it was perfectly tenable that Mary Pickford spent afternoons cavorting on the lawns of Pickfair in her ball gowns. After all, this was thirties Hollywood, and she was one of its legendary queens. Pickford lived out her life in this dream house.

signed Googie's, a coffee shop on Sunset Boulevard with glass walls and an aerodynamic tilted red roof, he effectively launched the pervasive goofy-coffee-shop-look of the fifties, known as Googie architecture. Coffee shops and drive-ins throughout the city were fitted with angled ceilings, prows, wings, pylons, and neon lights. And if that weren't enough to catch a motorist's eye, there were also towering signs that could be read four lanes away.

Today, it's not surprising that artists and designers feel free to conceive of their private living spaces as resembling nothing ever seen before, not even in L.A. The results are an expression in architecture and design that may be depicted in cinematic terms or simply in highly personal and creative ones.

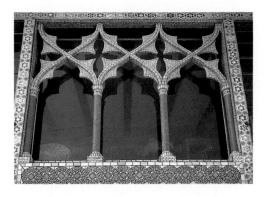

EHLING HOUSE

FAR LEFT: This enchanting abode represents the lifework of Hollywood studio technician George Ehling, and is the anything-but-humble home he created for his wife, Ivenia, and son, Otto. Although it looks like an enchanted castle and has everything going for it but a moat and drawbridge, the house actually rises atop a hill overlooking the San Fernando Valley, where many of today's television and movie studios are located. The property is encircled with a fanciful mosaic retaining wall. ABOVE: The decorative arches erected across the picture window on the front of the house are Italian Gothic in spirit. "I've taken most of the Spanish out of the house," offers Ehling.

Old European cities have castles and palaces that give citizens a taste of yore, but in Hollywood the only castles are the creations of modern-day dreamers. Such is the case with George Ehling and his mosaic palace, which sits on a mountain overlooking the San Fernando Valley. Motorists passing on a much-traveled winding thoroughfare skid to the stop at the sight of mysterious gargoyles and "ancient" Roman mosaics peeking out from the hillside. When the entire structure comes into view, the collage of colors and patterns, all worked in vibrant mosaic tile, becomes apparent.

The entire stucco façade, as well as the retaining wall of this 1920s Mediterranean chateau—actually, a large two-story house—is completely sheathed with thousands of tiles, each of which Ehling cut by hand and laid himself. Even before the exterior was complete, Ehling set to work

LEFT: A detail of the retaining wall shows the intricacy of Ehling's work. His mosaics are composed entirely of tile-store throwaways, which he "scrounges" from Dumpsters. BELOW LEFT: When Ehling worked on the movie *Murder by Death*, he made molds of the breakaway plaster gargoyles that were used on one of the sets and then recast the figures in concrete to stand watch over his house. Elsewhere around the house is a plaster cast of the head of the madonna from the movie *Exorcist II: The Heretic* and copies of corbels that appeared in a hotel scene in *The Natural*. The mosaic medallion over the front door is a Roman-style self-portrait. BELOW, CENTER: In Ehling's zeal, he lets nothing go to waste, including a forgotten toilet, which now functions as an outdoor cactus plant stand. BELOW, FAR LEFT: Ehling's handiwork is even apparent on a miniature castle complete with turrets, which has been usurped by a family feline. RIGHT: In the entrance, a grand staircase is punctuated with only a few choice tiles, and these, produced by Malibu Potteries, came with the house. The stairwell still has its original picture window.

on the walls, ceilings, and floors inside. He even tiled the doghouse and has started work on an outside shower and steam room.

Not surprisingly, this folly belongs to a motion-picture studio carpenter and prop maker with a flair for the dramatic. Ehling studied the craft of mosaics in Italy and was particularly inspired by the intricate ancient Roman designs he observed as he learned the Old World process. He calls his tile work an obsession, toils seven days a week on this epic project, and admits that the house will probably never stop evolving.

LEFT: Romanesque
arches add to the theat-
ricality of the house's
interior. On one side of
the arches, which Ehl-
ing constructed and
then paved with mosa-
ics, is the master bed-
room and, a half story
below, the living room.
RIGHT: In the living
room, a pair of Spanish
Baroque chairs look,
fittingly, like thrones.
Overhead are Roman-
style mosaic portraits
inspired by those at
Aquileia, an ancient Ro-
man city destroyed by
Attila. Appropriately,
Ehling refers to the
space as the "Aquileia
Room."

ABOVE: A passageway
off the dining room
holds a beautiful mosaic
bowl of flowers.

LEFT: The small master
bathroom is one of the
most exciting rooms in
the house. The geomet-
ric Cosmati-style mosa-
ics, typical of Italian
Romanesque buildings,
are employed from
floor to ceiling. Yet
even in this room there
are signs that the house
is a work in progress:
Ehling has yet to com-
plete the far column to
the right of the sink.

COPELAND HOUSE

Nobody knows how or why the so-called Mosque House came to be built or, for that matter, who designed it. It stands to reason that it was built by someone with a fertile imagination, so legend goes that it was a Hollywood producer. With its tiled minarets and domes and Moorish window treatments, the 1929-ish building overlooking Silver Lake was irresistible to John Copeland, who recently bought and refurbished it.

Copeland, who is curator and landscape specialist at the majestic Virginia Robinson Estate and Gardens in Beverly Hills, set out to amplify the witty details of this four-level, one-of-a-kind early Los Angeles folly. Repeating the same vibrant colors as in the existing tiles, he painted the entry walk, the exterior stairs, the bordered doors, and the windows in fanciful Islamic motifs, and added Watts-

Tower-esque cracked tile treatments to the otherwise standard kitchen. As if in sync with the house's original designer, Copeland's master stroke in the central courtyard is his trickling tile fountain set against a deep lavender wall lush with fiery fuchsia and orange bougainvillea.

Copeland's flair for the dramatic continues inside. The living room, with its junk-shop torches perched on the fluid mantel, looks like something out of a Rudolph Valentino movie. The juxtaposition of classic fifties furniture found in flea markets, early Los Angeles pottery, and copper sconces made by his own hand is further testimony to his eye for the unusual.

LEFT: A wrought-iron window grate is a resting place for a gardening hat, while a potted garden is fashioned from colorful Bauer containers. BELOW LEFT: An L.A. landscape dominated by a towering Mexican fan palm is viewed through a curvaceous Islamic archway leading to an upstairs patio. Inside the arch is a Mexican wrought-iron chair and a drip-glazed jardiniere, while poised in the background is a pot that Copeland embellished with mosaics. FAR LEFT: Copeland's use of strong color and judicious decoration enlivens a garden door. RIGHT: Beneath the gilded dome is the formal dining room, which offers a panoramic view of the Silver Lake neighborhood. The dining-room chairs and table were designed by Heywood Wakefield in the fifties. The pottery is early Catalina. Seen above the door is the broken-tile work Copeland created for the kitchen.

RIGHT: The living room is dominated by the house's original gold-tile-trimmed fireplace, on which Copeland has perched a pair of old torches. The home-owner decorated the hearth in black and gold. Seating is provided by one of Charles Eames's classic molded plywood chairs and an armchair slipcovered in black cotton duck. The turquoise pottery is all Bauer. BELOW RIGHT: Veering far from Moorish inspiration, a vignette in Copeland's bedroom includes a garage-sale chest and a Mexican *equipales* chair. Copeland found the American folk painting at Pasadena's Rose Bowl flea market. BELOW: Hardware-store springs are used to secure the goods stored on Copeland's kitchen shelves. The colorful display includes water pitchers, serving pieces, and plates by Russel Wright, Padre, Bauer, Catalina, and Hall.

RIGHT: With the original Moorish-style stained-glass windows in place in the breakfast room, little else is needed to enliven this room, where a white Catalina vase holds a single well-chosen leaf. Masks from Mexico are lined up above a simple painted sideboard. BELOW: More unusual seating is provided by a new wave chair, designed by Michele De Lucchi for Italy's Memphis group, and by a fifties chair by Norman Cherner. The forties sideboard holds a Moroccan lamp.

NIEMI/KLEIN HOUSE

LEFT: Sheila Klein and Ries Niemi barbecue in their side yard four out of seven nights each week, so their outdoor dining space has to be as idiosyncratic as their home's interior. Niemi, whose sculptures are often as functional as they are artistic, employed steel and steel reinforcing rods to construct his "Profile Bench," the seating unit in the foreground. From the branches of the coral tree that shades their patio, a crownlike chandelier of painted steel and colored light bulbs goes to work when the sun goes

down. The dining table was designed by architect Norman Millar. On top of the table sits "Eyelash," one of Klein's steel sculptures. The drinking glasses are made by L.A.'s Fine Line Studios. **Top:** Niemi's stick figures form a fence that is painted fluorescent orange, in stark contrast to the couple's jacaranda-

tree-blue house. **ABOVE:** Passersby can't help but pause to absorb the inventiveness at the Niemi/Klein house— even the front gate is a new take on functional art. The gate and grill-work on all windows and doors are the designs of metal artist Gale McCall and were executed by Niemi in his studio.

T ake an ordinary buttoned-up L.A. bungalow built in the twenties and add two nonconformists, and the result is a quirky mix of fun and function, ordinary and extraordinary. After completely gutting and remodeling their 800-square-foot "mini-estate," as they call it, metal sculptor Ries Niemi and his wife, artist Sheila Klein, merged his and her art forms on walls, floors, and windows, as well as on the fence that encircles their corner lot.

So fond is Niemi of wrought iron and rebar, the steel reinforcing rods that he uses for decoration and function, that the couple named their firstborn son Rebar. Using these metals, he and artist Gale McCall transformed ordinary window grates into primitive loops and lines that animate the exterior of the house. The playful orange stick-figure fence Niemi designed closes with a metal gate that looks like stretched animal hide branded with the street address.

Klein is one of the young local artists commissioned to create public art for a Hollywood Boulevard stop of Los Angeles's much-heralded new Metro Rail mass-transit system. In her home, she displays her whimsical oversized sculptures on the white walls and, working with artist Linda Beaumont, put a twist on the traditional ceramic-tiled fireplace in the living room by using a pattern of small hexagonal tiles typically found in bathrooms.

With the hammer-and-bulb light fixtures, the chandelier in the garden, the "T-shirt-and-shorts chair," the giant steel-and-linoleum earring dangling on a wall—this house is clearly the home of people who wrap their lives in art.

FAR LEFT: When the couple's son, Rebar, was born, Niemi designed this rocker out of the child's namesake material and inscribed the seat with his name and the date of his birth. Klein created the two large sculptures, as well as the small table on the floor, which she assembled from high heels and a Chinese dice table. Two crowns are displayed on the stacking tables: on the top shelf, a Jivaro Indian feather crown and on the bottom shelf, a sculpture by Gale McCall. BELOW LEFT: No flying intruders will bug the couple even on the hottest Southern California nights. Black mosquito netting covers the bed from ceiling to floor. The quilt was made from surgical canvas by Carl Smoll. The bed was designed and constructed by Niemi, and the hanging sculptures above it, "Fatal Hook and Cavity," are by Klein. BOTTOM LEFT: Niemi's stick figures and Klein's artful constructions are at work throughout the living room. Their "T-Shirt and Shorts" chair is an experimental study in Formica. BELOW: The spidery light fixture, which is a collaborative work by the homeowners, brightens the dining area, as does the painting by McCall and the "Futurustic" message art by Phil Garner.

LAWRENCE/
SANDUM HOUSE

FAR LEFT: Even in a city where anything goes, the Lawrence/Sandum House is one of a kind. Although the structure of the building itself is plain wrap, the paint job is anything but. Artist Jim Lawrence covered every inch of its surface with personal tattoos that have "secret references," he says, but he was strongly influenced by African and Bornean tribal tattoos as well as by African and Oceanic art and architecture. A cheery front-porch garden adds a domestic touch. TOP LEFT: Lawrence painted the wrought-iron bench, and daughter Alexandria was assigned the job of decorating the chair. The furniture gives the front garden an unexpected sense of formal grace. The cracked concrete floor is sprinkled with broken tiles. ABOVE LEFT: No wall has been left untattooed. Behind the expressive garage doors is Lawrence's studio.

The hand of an artist whose raw, jagged sculptures often shock the emotions has fashioned a living environment that's at once surprisingly homey and unquestionably provocative. On a block of cookie-cutter stucco houses, his "tattooed" clapboard cottage, though hidden from the street, is a startling statement. Painter and sculptor Jim Lawrence says the transformation of the house he shares with his wife, Cherie Sandum, and daughter, Alexandria, began unintentionally. He started constructing furniture that would function in tiny quarters, and painted a small coffee table in the living room with black and white symbols inspired by tribal tattoos. Once he finished the table, he continued the motif on posts surrounding the front porch. Then he "tattooed" the entire house. "I was so excited once I did the four posts that I carried it through. It took less than three weeks to

ABOVE: Lawrence's tattooing project began in the living room with the coffee table he built, seen here in the center of the room, with an elegant chair by Philippe Starck pulled up alongside it. Lawrence's own large-scale sculptures are displayed, along with African masks and a Chinese garden stool. RIGHT: In Alexandria's bedroom, a wall is dominated by an array of art. Lawrence made the side table, while the violin-motif quilt was stitched by her grandmother. TOP RIGHT: In the dining area, Lawrence designed a table, cut on an angle, which not only allows for easy access to the kitchen but seats three perfectly. On the wall is one of Lawrence's wire, resin, and fabric sculptures, entitled "Vampire." FAR RIGHT: Another table designed by the artist is on view in the entry area.

paint the whole house," he recalls. While the effect could have been ominous, Lawrence's choice of bright pastels gives the house a certain naïveté. Even eleven-year-old Alexandria shares in the joy of it.

The house is the perfect "gallery" for Lawrence's large- and small-scale works. His artful inspirations appear in every room—hand-painted on the kitchen cabinets, and, in the form of large sculptures, hanging from the ceiling in the dining area and perched alongside the sofa and chairs in the living room.

An intimate and totally original outdoor retreat is hidden behind the home. Clover grows in the cracks of a quaint broken-concrete-and-tile path. The tiny trail leads to a drought-resistant garden, where large succulents flourish year 'round. Along a side wall, broken pieces of pottery create a colorful tableau. Whimsical garden furniture hand-painted by Lawrence and Alexandria provide seating and infuse the space with charm. Very little of L.A.'s precious water is needed to bring this wonderful environment to life.

LEFT: Waking up at Gronk's place is like entering a dream world instead of leaving one behind. Dynamic color explodes everywhere, including on the footboard of the bed, which looks like a page from a psychedelic comic book. Once used as part of a stage set for a local theater production called *Performance Anxiety*, the vividly painted backdrop puts television on a pedestal, a tongue-in-cheek comment by the resident artist. Gronk painted the huge acrylic canvas on the wall, entitled "Rise and Kill," in 1990 as part of an exhibit devoted to zombies. In dramatic contrast are the romantic roses Gronk splashes in all sizes throughout his living space. TOP LEFT: Without walls to delineate rooms (except for the bath), the industrial aerie is luxuriously wide open and serves as both Gronk's living quarters and his studio. The massive black-and-chrome chair seen here is by Los Angeles furniture designer Herb Sandoval. In the far corner is Gronk's larger-than-life cutout figure, "Wrestler." ABOVE LEFT: Gronk's urban garden consists of a few potted succulents that thrive on the tar-paper deck. By simply climbing out a window, he can easily admire his prickly crop or reflect on the blue skies.

The downtown loft of the Los Angeles artist who goes by the singular name of Gronk is a private oasis with no suggestion of the gritty urban street scene on the sidewalks below—thanks to the rooftop deck that the loft's windows look out upon. While Gronk takes inspiration from the city and people around him, his combination home and studio is his personal refuge. Near this large former warehouse, neighbors are few and far between, and he can paint without distraction for hours.

Gronk's world looks like a giant three-dimensional cartoon. His huge paintings and whimsical stage sets form the backdrop for—and, in the case of his bed, which was once a stage prop, actually serve as—his furniture. He leaves balloons and confetti from past celebrations strewn around as an ever-present reminder of good times.

Gronk, who grew up in East Los Angeles and received little formal art training, is recognized as one of the foremost young Hispanic artists in the city. His early work was on display in a coffeehouse when it was spotted by a curator from the Los Angeles Museum of Contemporary Art. He was then one of thirty Chicano artists featured in an exhibition of Hispanic art in the United States at the Los Angeles County Museum of Art, and his pieces have since been on display all over the world. While his strong imagery dominates every corner of his loft, his works also share wall and floor space with art made by friends who also call Los Angeles home.

BOTTOM: "Clark," a Gronkian take on Superman, seems to be in a hurry to change in the shower. Many of the works on the walls are pieces Gronk now collects from art shows at coffeehouses. A tank-top assemblage features Tomato DuPlenty's "Blue Boy" (1989) and a display of trinkets and toys, all ringed by a necklace of skulls. **RIGHT:** A red-and-black Formica-topped grooming table in the bathroom comes complete with a high-heeled ruby slipper to match.

FAR LEFT, ABOVE: Gronk says he survives very well without a traditional kitchen. A motel refrigerator holds enough cream for his coffee and keeps the mineral water cold. Rather than cook his own breakfast, Gronk makes a daily pilgrimage to Clifton's Silver Spoon Cafeteria, a downtown eatery built in 1922, where he reads the paper and listens to other people's conversations "for inspiration—then I come home and paint." In the place where others might put a kitchen table, Gronk plunks Steve LaPonsie's two-dimensional artwork, complete with meal and diners. LaPonsie also painted the "Tumbling Dice" sign. The cottage cheese container is a found object. Gronk added the fixed "light beams" that radiate from the lamp on the counter and also surrounded his 1989 "Coffee Cup" with roses that he painted directly on the wall. The blackheart collage above the pantry shelves is by Patssi Valdez. LEFT: A festive party mood can get deadly after a while, or at least that's what this black-tie couple seems to be indicating. Her gun is shooting a steady stream of blue Christmas lights, and he appears to have gotten her message. The pair were originally conceived for a Day of the Dead celebration at the old L.A. Theater Center.

Avant-Garde

Symbolic of new beginnings,

Los Angeles is also a

frontier for new architecture.

Architect Frank Gehry

has called Southern

Traditions

California "a context that

creates freedom," and

that has been true since the

turn of the century. With-

out centuries of architectural

precedents, L.A. is a fertile

breeding ground for new,

constantly evolving design.

LEFT: Avant-garde took on new form in 1991 with the clean but colorful geometry of Eric and Vanessa Hansen's residence overlooking the San Fernando Valley. "We like to add potent color at places of importance," explains the architect, longtime modernist Donald C. Hensman of Buff, Smith & Hensman. TOP RIGHT: Richard J. Neutra's International-style hillside house for Philip and Leah Lovell, known as Health House, drew worldwide attention to Los Angeles in the twenties. The privately owned residence remains one of the city's modernist gems. RIGHT: A few years later, and on flatter terrain, Neutra built this house for one of his many movie-industry clients, Edward Kaufman. Today, it is owned by Academy Award–winning visual effects designer Richard Edlund (see page 265).

9

Modern architecture was and still is created by architects on the edge for people living on the edge. The edge can be interpreted in several ways: geographically, Los Angeles is at the edge of the continent. Psychologically, there's the looming sense of calamity that comes from living at the mercy of earthquakes, fires, and landslides. Creatively, architects from Irving Gill in the teens to the Young Turks of today, take chances using forms, techniques, and building materials that others have overlooked—or never dreamed of. This on-the-edge mentality separates the Los Angeles modern contingent from the more tradition-bound architects in the rest of the country. And since much of the city's startling avant-garde design is associated with residences, certainly willing private patrons are a driving force. These clients not only have money to spend but also possess a free spirit to match that of the forward-thinking architects to whom they give the green light.

Considered L.A.'s first modernist, Gill, who had worked with Frank Lloyd Wright in Adler & Sullivan's Chicago office in the 1890s, was stripping Spanish Colonial, Mission, and Pueblo architecture to the bones just after the turn of the century. But Gill wasn't for everyone, and was rarely imitated, becoming "almost a prophet without honor," as David Gebhard and Robert Winter point out in their popular reference book *Architecture in Los Angeles: A Compleat Guide*. Gill's modern masterpiece, the Dodge House in West Hol-

BELOW: The West Hollywood house Rudolph M. Schindler designed for himself and his wife, Pauline, was a unique foray into casual living and experimental building materials. Today, it is open to the public. BOTTOM: Poised above a sweeping city view, Pierre Koenig's aerie, known as Stahl House, was the twenty-second residence built for *Arts & Architecture* magazine's Case Study House Program. All of the walls on the back side of the house, facing the pool area, are glass, thus reinforcing the indoor-outdoor relationship.

lywood (1916), was a collection of cubistic volumes broken by irregularly placed windows surrounding a central courtyard and fountain. Dodge House, paneled inside with elegant wood, was disrespectfully razed by the city in 1969.

During his brief Los Angeles sojourn, Frank Lloyd Wright explored Mayan themes and precast concrete block construction, an evolution of his Midwestern Prairie Style. While he built only six houses here, it was via Wright that the International Style was introduced to the region. He hired Rudolph M. Schindler, a young Austrian architect, to assist him as construction supervisor on Aline Barnsdall's Hollyhock House in 1920 (see page 259). Schindler never left. And it was at Schindler's urging that his Viennese friend and fellow Wright disciple, Richard J. Neutra, moved here in 1925. Neutra and his wife, Dione, settled in with Schindler and his wife, Pauline, into an iconoclastic "double house" in West Hollywood, with a communal kitchen and outdoor sleeping rooms, which Schindler designed. The Schindler House (1921) merged concrete slab walls with sliding glass, redwood, and canvas, and created a casual yet experimental indoor-outdoor environment where flowing spaces open onto a large garden with exterior fireplaces.

Schindler's design for a vacation house in Newport Beach for Philip and Leah Lovell, a glass-and-concrete edifice balanced on piers (1926), became an important modern paragon. But when the Lovells' larger commission for their home in the Hollywood Hills was won by Neutra, the result was the dissolution of the two architects' friendship. Neutra, however, created what is considered one of the world's seminal modern structures, and its construction marked the turning point in his career, according to Thomas S. Hines in *Richard Neutra and the Search for Modern Archi-*

tecture. The so-called Lovell Health House (1929), angled into a steep hillside, was the first completely steel-framed residence in America. Machine-made casement windows, concrete, glass, metallic paint, and Model-T Ford headlights used as interior

lighting created a striking image for the industrial age. The Health House sealed Neutra's reputation as a modern American master, and his fame spread to the Bauhaus in Dessau, Germany. Indeed, the Los Angeles work of Schindler and Neutra in the twenties predated American buildings by Ludwig Mies van der Rohe and Walter Gropius.

As the leading West Coast modernist, Neutra continued to build houses, primarily in Los Angeles, as well as apartment buildings, factories, stores, theaters, office buildings, and schools throughout the thirties, forties, fifties, and sixties. So important was his work that in 1949 Neutra's face graced the cover of *Time* magazine. During the Depression, he was kept busy with important commissions from movie-industry people, including homes for actress Anna Sten and her husband, director Eugene Frenke (1934), director Josef von Sternberg (1935), and writer-producer-director Albert Lewin (1938), and an office building for Universal-International Pictures (1932).

BELOW: Frank Lloyd Wright's monumental and exotic Hollyhock House (see page 259) was one of six exceptional residences the architect built in the city. Standing in the gardens, visitors can see Wright's Ennis House, a structure built a few years later, which was also strongly influenced by pre-Columbian themes. ABOVE: Frank Gehry's startling renovation of his plain Dutch Colonial home incurred the ire of many of his neighbors when it was completed. An oblique window set in a wall of corrugated sheet metal is seen here.

Other modernists working in Los Angeles before World War II included J. R. Davidson, Frank Lloyd Wright's son Lloyd, and Kem Weber, as well as Raphael Soriano, Gregory Ain, and Harwell Harris, who worked in Neutra's studio.

During the Depression and war years, with few buildings to design, local architects had time to absorb, contemplate, and interpret the ideas introduced by modernism and to study ways to incorporate advanced materials and construction techniques developed for wartime use. With the help of a local magazine, *Arts & Architecture*, that period of deliberation soon resulted in progressive design approaches to the postwar housing shortage.

The magazine's publisher, John Entenza, was intent on pioneering concepts that would modernize homes for the masses and soon launched the daring Case Study House Program. In 1945, he commissioned eight architects to devise prototypes for two- and three-bedroom, two-bath homes for the typical postwar family. By the time Cary Grant starred in *Mr. Blandings Builds His Dream House*, in 1948, the first six experimental dwellings had been erected, landscaped, and furnished, and more than 350,000 house-hungry Angelenos had toured them. The Case Study House Program continued until 1967, when the magazine folded. By that time, a total of twenty-four Case Study projects had been built.

Since most of the 1940s Case Study houses were constructed of wood posts and beams, the steel-and-glass structures of the fifties were the real technological innovations. Perhaps the most important of these homes are the two-story house Charles and Ray Eames built for themselves (1949) and Pierre Koenig's Stahl House (1959–60). Hugging its Pacific Palisades cliff and shielded from view by a grove of eucalyptus

trees, the Eames house and its separate art studio sit like an unmatched pair of boxes with steel ribs and geometric splashes of red, blue, black, and white.

Koenig's glass pavilion cantilevers from a West Hollywood hillside to take full advantage of the site's panoramic city view. Vast walls of glass jut into space, integrating interior and exterior spaces, and concrete foot bridges span sections of the swimming pool and lead to the main entrance of the house.

Among the other notable architects participating in the Case Study House Program were Thornton Abell, Conrad Buff III, Davidson, Craig Ellwood, Donald Hensman, A. Quincy Jones, Edward Killingsworth, Neutra, Eero Saarinen, Soriano, Calvin Straub, and William Wurster.

Although totally modern in concept, the Case Study houses never achieved Entenza's goal of revolutionizing mass housing. Steel-and-glass construction, though state-of-the-art, proved to be too difficult to execute and too expensive for low-budget residential projects. However, architects throughout the world were influenced by the Case Study Program, which reinforced and expanded on modernist tenets through advanced technology. As Reyner Banham points out in *Blueprints for Modern Living,* "international architects also went on to translate these concepts into huge industrial facilities, setting the stage for the 'high tech' age."

ABOVE LEFT: Case Study House number eight, the home of designers Charles and Ray Eames, was a study in geometry and color executed in prefabricated industrial parts. In contrast to its stark exterior, the couple filled the interior with a profusion of folk art, dolls, textiles, and plants, as well as with their own furniture designs. **ABOVE:** For architect Michael Rotondi, his family home is an ongoing test laboratory for his ideas (see page 285). Here, a waxed steel tower and retaining wall rise from a sloping site.

Except for the excitement generated by the *Arts & Architecture* experiment, the world paid little attention to the residential architecture of Los Angeles in the fifties and sixties. Important East Coast modern architects had little interest in trying to win commissions here. Architectural critics complained that the city was growing too fast, with no thought to design, and snickered at ticky-tacky housing tracts that had supplanted orange groves in the suburbs. Ever-present was the informal ranch house modeled after architect Cliff May's rambling styles, which suited the Southern California lifestyle so well.

But the space age had begun, and a few architects were trying to shape the future. John Lautner, who had come from Michigan in the thirties to study with Frank Lloyd Wright, engaged in structural gymnastics with his Chemosphere House (1960), an octagonal module supported on a concrete pedestal affixed to one of the Hollywood hills. Although it was his most publicized building, Chemosphere was no more radically original than the other seventy houses Lautner designed in Southern California.

At the same time, A. Quincy Jones, who would become dean of the School of Architecture and Fine Arts at the University of Southern California in 1975, took the essential elements of May's ranch houses and incorporated them into trendsetting modern homes for the rich. Unfortunately, the graceful yet dramatic A-frame rooflines and huge, barnlike interior spaces he had carefully articulated were copied unsuccessfully by developers in housing tracts throughout the state.

Ray Kappe, who experimented in imaginative wood-and-glass structures, including his own multilevel "treehouse" in Rustic Canyon, founded the Southern California Institute of Architecture (SCI-Arc) in 1972, which today is considered one of the world's most innovative schools in its field.

In the 1970s, the work of Charles Moore and Frank Gehry shook the steel foundations of modernism by throwing out the rules. Moore's first L.A. commission, the Burns House in Pacific Palisades (1974), is a complex, shed-roofed structure recalling his earlier Sea Ranch condominiums in Northern California (1965). Soaked in bright Mexican colors, the house makes reference to the city's Spanish Colonial past with a luxuriantly planted, walled, and tiled entrance court. Moore also created dramatic imagery with a nod to the visual tricks of Hollywood movie sets by juxtaposing two-dimensional façades to define another private courtyard and pool. Shortly after its completion, Moore, for-

BELOW: Perched in the Hollywood Hills, John Lautner's futuristic Chemosphere House is as compelling a sight today as it was when it was built, more than thirty years ago. A funicular still carries residents up the precipitous hillside. BOTTOM: Early in the century, Dodge House was considered a prime example of Irving Gill's spare new architectural vocabulary. He reinterpreted Hispanic and Indian architecture, and the resulting structure spoke of the cultural past while bringing the region into the future.

merly chairman of the department of architecture at the University of California, Berkeley, and the dean of Yale's School of Architecture and Planning, moved to Los Angeles to teach architecture at UCLA. In other commissions, including those for private homes and the Beverly Hills Civic Center (1990), Moore continues his exploration of historic allusions, eclecticism, free use of color, and whimsy.

Frank Gehry, by contrast, "tore down" traditional notions of design by demolishing walls, exposing raw studs and plywood, and wrapping corrugated sheet metal around the façade of his own house (1978), once an undistinguished bungalow. By elevating inexpensive building supplies to valuable, integral design elements—partly as an intellectual challenge and partly out of economic necessity—and by playing with angles and space, Gehry demands that viewers accept a more eclectic definition of architecture. Today Gehry's international success and multi-million-dollar commissions for museums, office buildings, and Los Angeles's Walt Disney Concert Hall require him to incorporate the same dear materials he once shunned, yet he continues to be an architectural renegade.

In the eighties and early nineties, L.A. is still spawning explorations into new forms and ideas. The city has matured into a vibrant economic and cultural capital, attracting internationally acclaimed architects, such as Arata Isozaki, Richard Meier, and I. M. Pei, to embellish its uniquely sprawling skyline. A new generation of local architects, designers, colorists, and craftspeople are building houses that both recall the past and speak to the future. They, like the avant-garde masters before them, find L.A. fertile ground for their new expressions.

HOLLYHOCK HOUSE

LEFT: The dining room of Frank Lloyd Wright's historic Hollyhock House features the original furniture designed by the architect. The hollyhock motif, which is carved on the backs of the chairs and on the base of the hexagonal table, is also interpreted in the trim of the wood paneling. In this room, the walls and furniture are crafted of rare *genizero* wood from the South and Central American *guanacaste* tree, which has a grain similar to that of mahogany. The bilevel leaded-glass windows were designed to provide two vistas, one of the mountains, for people standing in the room, and one of the gardens, for those seated at the table. **ABOVE:** In the garden adjacent to the main entrance to the house, hollyhocks still flourish today. From the gardens, visitors can enjoy a panoramic view of the city.

Frank Lloyd Wright's extraordinary Hollyhock House, completed in 1921, was the first of many important houses the architect designed in Los Angeles.

Bohemian oil heiress Aline Barnsdall offered Wright a chance to experiment beyond the range—geographically and stylistically—of his Midwestern Prairie School houses. Working in Los Angeles, he could also leave behind the personal tragedies that had befallen him, including the death of his companion and two of her children, who were murdered by a servant in a fire that virtually destroyed their home in Taliesin, his Wisconsin retreat.

Wright was influenced by pre-Columbian architecture and used it as a point of departure at Hollyhock. At the house, on Olive Hill in Los Angeles, Wright was able to embrace all the romantic notions of California living. He built it around a great courtyard and reflecting pool, encircled with roof gardens. Glass doors provided access to gardens on all sides of the house and capitalized on a sweeping 360-degree view of the city.

Constructed of a wood frame, hollow tile, and stucco, the house got its name from its concrete adornments, styl-

LEFT: A matching pair of tables, built around two seven-foot oak light towers, project from the backs of two massive couches in the living room. The large open space demanded furniture that was as imposing as the room. Wright even designed the room's original carpeting, draperies, and upholstery, which were later re-created for the room as it stands today. The Oriental screen belonged to Aline Barnsdall, who lived in the house for only six years.

ized versions of Barnsdall's favorite flower. The hollyhock motif also appears inside on carpets and concrete columns and run along the backs of Wright-designed dining-room chairs, which remain in the house today. In the gardens, yellow and pink hollyhocks still bloom.

Rooms are designed to flow into one another, establishing a feeling of wide open spaces. Perhaps the only nod to the city's rampant Mediterranean Revival architecture (which Wright openly hated) is that all major rooms had direct access to the central courtyard. Since Wright was spending much of his time in Japan working on the Imperial Hotel, he assigned architect Rudolph Schindler as construction supervisor at Hollyhock. Schindler went on to design a wading pool and pergola with the assistance of Richard Neutra.

In 1927, Barnsdall gave the house, along with one guest residence, to the city of Los Angeles with the stipulation that it be used for arts and recreation purposes. Today, the house and its grounds are known as Barnsdall Art Park.

BELOW: In the dining room, storage cabinets for silver and linen flank the double doors that lead to the kitchen. Beyond is a long, narrow kitchen with a pitched ceiling that still looks surprisingly contemporary.

TOP AND ABOVE: Because Wright believed that it was the heart of the home, Hollyhock's impressive fireplace is the focal point of the living room. Made of cast concrete, its abstract bas-relief is inset with small gold tiles. Integrating the elements of nature to the fullest extent, Wright positioned a small pool surrounding the hearth and designed a large leaded-glass skylight above the fireplace. The room opens onto outdoor gardens at each end. The sofa, tables, and light towers in the living room were recently reproduced from Wright's original designs.

RIGHT: Wright favored highly stylized forms for his California houses of the 1920s. Viewed from the side garden, a repeating geometric shape defines the back wall of a niche in the main entryway to the house. The niche was originally designed to accommodate an Oriental sculpture. Today, grape ivy spills over the wall. Hollyhock House has been open to the public since 1976.

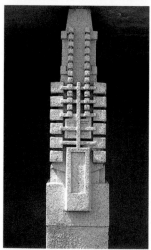

ABOVE: Wright translated the showy hollyhock stalk into sophisticated geometric ornamentation, reminiscent of Mayan motifs. Cast in concrete on the exterior, woven into the carpet, or carved in wood, Wright's hollyhock became the well-known symbol of this monumental work.

ABOVE: Aline Barnsdall's only child, her daughter, Sugar Top, was four when they moved into Hollyhock House. This enclosed porch is off Sugar Top's bedroom. There were originally two doors providing access to the gardens, but over the years the design was altered. The leaded glass, based on Wright's design, was installed during the 1974–76 renovation.

RIGHT: When the Barnsdalls lived in the house, these private gardens, off the original guest bedrooms, were filled with hollyhocks. In fact, a photo in Aline's personal album shows the gardens dense with the vibrantly colored stalks. Visitors standing in the circular courtyard today can look through gardens to the gallery and pergola and beyond into the central courtyard.

KAUFMAN HOUSE

A few years after Richard Neutra gained worldwide attention for his Lovell Health House in the Hollywood Hills, he was commissioned by Edward Kaufman, a composer at MGM Studios, to design this two-story house in Westwood. Almost fifty years after it was finished, Kaufman's house (1937), with its large expanses of windows, generous interior spaces, and well-proportioned cabinetry, appealed to the sensibilities of another professional involved with filmmaking. Its present owner, Richard Edlund, received Academy Awards in the visual effects category for all three *Star Wars* movies and for *Raiders of the Lost Ark*.

"The house has a sophisticated flow to it," says Edlund, who bought it in 1983 along with many of the original furnishings, designed by Neutra himself. Though Edlund added a swimming pool of his own design, he worked with the architect's plans to restore the house to its original luster.

Elegant Neutra signatures include the copper-and-chrome architectural trim upstairs and down, interior walls of Philippine mahogany, large mirrors, glass bricks, and metal doors. Edlund's collections of nineteenth-century Japanese ceramics, bronzes, and ivory complement the clean lines.

ABOVE: The living room is a fine example of Neutra's aesthetic, as it features all the original built-in furniture. Banquettes upholstered in a Bauhaus design abut the fireplace, which has a polished copper surround and a terrazzo hearth. The copper, glass, and chrome andirons were made for the house. The Neutra-designed coffee table carries out the copper theme he planned throughout the house's ground floor. The pottery on display is both nineteenth-century Japanese and California art pottery of the thirties. On the piano is a Chinese Kuan Yin goddess of mercy. **MIDDLE:** In the wood-paneled library, a Neutra-designed copper-and-leather chair is pulled up to a built-in desk. **RIGHT:** In the library, Neutra's penchant for built-in furniture is shown in a wall of bookshelves and cabinetry made of Philippine mahogany. Here, Edlund displays Japanese ivory carvings and bronzes as well as ivory tusks. **FAR RIGHT:** A sleek staircase curves to the second-floor bedrooms, where lighting fixtures, furniture, and trims are all fashioned of chrome, in contrast to the copper motif Neutra conceived for the downstairs. A Japanese Shigaraki ceramic jar rests in a niche.

FAR LEFT: By mingling family heirlooms and contemporary art pieces, Diantha Lebenzon has softened the raw edges of the living room in her Frank Gehry house. Next to a comfortable old armchair is a side table fashioned from palm frond and marble by Los Angeles artist Jim

LEBENZON HOUSE

Ganzer. The sculptural dining-room table by L.A. artist Billy Al Bengston is accompanied by a set of chairs from a forties cruise ship. The painting above the table is by Roger Herman. Peeking through the kitchen is an Andy Warhol cow. ABOVE: After two drastic remodeling jobs, the residence has changed dramatically from its earliest incarnation as a plain stucco house.

At the same time that Frank Gehry was making rule-breaking advances in architecture with his now-well-known Santa Monica residence (1978), he was also redesigning this shapeless fifties stucco house in Hollywood.

While leaving the original exterior walls intact, Gehry built a new stucco façade in front of the house, creating a functional shell that houses a new stairwell and a front hall. This early example of Gehry's foray into deconstructivism was built by the architect as a speculative real estate venture. When film producer Diantha Lebenzon bought the house, she hired John Clagett, a former Gehry associate, to add a master bedroom suite on top of the existing structure. The new room has a dramatic vista that includes Beverly Hills, Los Angeles, and, on a clear day, the Pacific Ocean.

Lebenzon's elegant antiques and contemporary art make for startling juxtapositions with exposed beams and tie rods. "It's very easy to live here," says the owner, who was more accustomed to traditional environments before wrapping herself in a Gehry. She worked with decorative arts historian Julia Winston to add soft touches to the house's hard lines and to add warmth where otherwise-cold building materials might have prevailed.

LEFT: In Lebenzon's office, a kitschy fifties bamboo desk and chair coexist with more staid Early American antiques, including a rocker and an armoire. The clock on the armoire plays music by Franz Schubert. The rug is a kilim. BELOW: Disparate collections are on view in an inviting seating area next to the living-room fireplace, including carved wood apostles from Italy, leather-bound editions of Shakespeare, and contemporary art by Willem de Kooning and Francesco Clemente. To the right, a broken Chinese Buddha rests on an English cabinet. In the den, to the left, is an oil painting in four sections by Roger Herman.

LEFT: Rich textiles and colors create a sense of luxury in the master bedroom despite the unfinished plywood walls. "What the house needed was a little warmth," says Lebenzon. Paisley shawls cover a Louis XVI chair and are draped over the bed, which has been dressed in a cotton muslin slipcover. Reflected in a mirror propped against the wall is a sofa swathed with Fortuny silk. The table in the foreground is Biedermeier and the rug is Chinese. BELOW: One of Lebenzon's more diminutive dogs finds a place to rest on a Federal love seat in the living room. Its refined lines are a surprising contrast to the building's original wood frame structure, exposed and left intact.

WARD HOUSE

FAR LEFT: Charles and Ramey Ward and their son, Milo, live in a peaceful retreat that recalls early California. Its colonnade echoes the eighteenth-century missions, yet its geometric lap pool and cascading waterfall inject a sense of the future. Charles Ward, the architectural designer who designed and built the complex, says their home is all about seclusion, "where people can live inside and outside and still be private." **BELOW LEFT:** As seen from the street, the house emanates a fortresslike quality. The concrete-and-wood structure sits squarely on a narrow lot in urban Venice.

An inconspicuous concrete wall is all that's apparent from the street. But once through the elaborate security system at the front door, architectural designer Charles Ward, his wife, Ramey, and their son, Milo, enter their private fantasy universe. A lushly landscaped path leads to the dramatic colonnade that separates the narrow rectangular house from a long lap pool edged with cascading ice plant and tall grasses.

In a city where front yards have so much appeal, this fortress-like environment is unusual, but Ward, inspired by Mediterranean walled houses, values having a refuge from the inner-city landscape. Unlike typical Los Angeles houses, which seem like fishbowls to Ward, his keeps a decidedly low street profile.

Ward calls his work the antithesis of the mass-produced architecture so prevalent today. He makes architectural allusions to the *corredores* of California missions, and to Mexican architect Luis Barragan's symbiosis of building and earth. In fact, Ward prizes minor imperfections. "I've always thought that old, abandoned buildings have a real beauty—the feeling of being left to decay. Once a factory is abandoned, it becomes so romantic," says Ward. To achieve his own form of "decay," he uses concrete and plaster in their natural states, so they can gracefully weather with age. The rough-hewn elements contrast with the rich, colorful textiles and contemporary art in the interior. Perhaps that's why this house seems so timeless, even though it is strikingly modern.

LEFT: The lightest and brightest room in the house is the master bedroom, in which double doors open onto a balcony overlooking the pool. Using Indian rugs, Italian tapestry fabric, and Guatemalan weavings, the Wards maintain an ethnic feeling. But for an L.A. twist, Ward also uses the room for his workouts and hangs a punching bag in one corner.

LEFT: Windows in this small bedroom were designed so the inhabitants can fully view the palm trees in this beachy neighborhood. Counterbalancing the straight lines of Ward's architecture are a round portrait by L.A. artist Michael Alatza, a curving ponyskin-covered chaise longue, the squiggling trunk of a ficus tree, and the circular knots in the high-sheen pine floor.

RIGHT: Light streams in through a lightwell that extends to the second-story skylight, casting a diffused glow on the dining room. The showpiece of the room is the Pennsylvania slate dining table Ward designed. On the walls is a suite of 1964 lithographs by Ellsworth Kelly. The wooden high chair with its woven seat is a family heirloom from the eighteenth century.

WINDWARD CIRCLE

BELOW LEFT: A façade marked by spiraling concrete-filled culvert pipe is a reference to the building's past, when it was a popular hotel and water from the Grand Canal splashed up onto its portico.

Architecture lovers have made the beachside community of Venice a mecca for viewing the many exceptional buildings here conceived by internationally acclaimed architects. Arata Isozaki was inspired to build a small artist's studio less than a block from the sand. Frank Gehry has created several multiple-family dwellings in the area. Two avant-garde spaces by the L.A. firm Morphosis are within blocks of each other.

LEFT: After architect Steven Ehrlich created the Arts Building in 1988 on Windward Circle in Venice, resident David Saltz requested that the designer incorporate a professional gym and a basketball court on the second floor, the same level that holds his home office. Perhaps the plan was to provide some outlet for physical release after mental exertion. Whatever the scheme, guests seem to gravitate there, and most can't resist shooting a few baskets.

Steven Ehrlich has designed three of the major buildings on Windward Circle, now a traffic roundabout but once the Grand Canal and heart of this historic little town. These structures, Ehrlich says, "aim to resurrect the energy of the past, rather than simply to replicate the historical." Surely Abbot Kinney, the businessman who developed Venice in 1905 as a center of high culture, would be pleased. Ehrlich's own office is housed in a building called Race Through the Clouds, on a site that once held a roller coaster (designed by A. F. Rosenheim in 1912) of the same name. Knowing that, viewers feel that the track of galvanized steel and neon that undulates around the building makes perfect sense. Across the circle, Ehrlich's Ace Market Place combines huge constructivist components—which make subtle reference to the earth movers that originally excavated the canals—to form the corner marquee of the retail center.

Ehrlich's only residential structure on the circle is the Arts Building, where David Saltz, a television producer, lives. The exterior, with its columns and narrow portico, is reminiscent of the Antlers Hotel, which once sat on the site. Inside, three stories of living space, which were conceived as three separate units, have been joined. Perhaps the most spectacular is the middle floor, which holds a professional gym and basketball court, where Saltz can shoot till the wee hours if he pleases. On the third level, the bedroom/bath suite is one huge room, complete with a cascading waterfall shower.

Top Left: The dining-cum-living room overlooks Windward Circle. Here, near the built-in espresso bar, a new Mexican iron table and chairs mix with the classic lines of chrome and leather modern furniture. The compact spiral staircase leads to the rooftop, where the Pacific Ocean fills the vista to the west. To the south are the Venice canals, where ducks and geese waddle on the shores. **Left:** A house where guests can step off the elevator and sink a hook shot is not your usual house. But for Ehrlich the challenge was to indulge Saltz's passion for his sport and create an in-novative living space. On each side of the hoop are monochrome canvases by Jeanine Chantilly. **Above:** As Ehrlich points out, this space "breaks down the common definitions most people have of sleeping, bathing, and lounging." Rather than build walls to block bath from bedroom, Ehrlich created one huge space, with the bed raised on a plat-form. Water falls from cantilevered steel to fill the open tub and Ja-cuzzi. **Right:** Indian slate surrounds the fire-place in the living room, a subtle contrast to Saltz's black and gray furniture.

LOMBARDI HOUSE

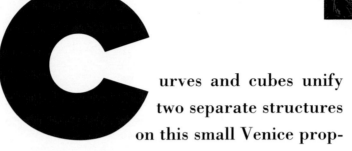

Curves and cubes unify two separate structures on this small Venice property. Using beautiful orange iron grilles as garage doors and blocks of ocher and white, architect Greg Lombardi dressed up what could have been a nondescript carport. In fact, the luxury cars parked inside become integral to the design of the transparent yet extremely secure garage.

ABOVE: Behind the garage, a spiral staircase leads to a guest apartment. From upstairs, guests get a bird's-eye view of the streets of Venice. Tropical plants flourish year round.

FAR LEFT: When architect Greg Lombardi designed his home on a narrow lot in Venice, the only practical way to achieve complete privacy was to put the garage in the front of the property, separating the main house from the street. But rather than overlook the aesthetic possibilities of a functional automobile storehouse, Lombardi exploited them. Gale McCall designed the vivid orange grillwork gates. The architect filled the driveway with "grasscrete," concrete pierced with holes so that ground cover can grow through it. The approach to the garage has become, in effect, a front garden, "a little jewel in the neighborhood," as Lombardi sees it. **ABOVE LEFT:** A reflecting pool and fountain add another design element to the courtyard garden.

This unusual approach is Lombardi's answer to making the most out of a functional space that entirely blocks the main house from view. Visitors enter the property through a matching grillwork gate and come upon the second "room," a tree-rimmed private garden flanked by the garage and the main house.

The house is a simple white box broken by five panels of glass, the center one framing double entry doors. Inside, more decorative grillwork—by Los Angeles artist Gale McCall—reappears in the living room, as a banister, here in the delicate green, and an asymmetrical black coffee table.

Lombardi, an L.A. native, says that with this house he has attempted to make sense of all the things around him. Though frankly incorporating tenets of International style architecture, he also makes reference to L.A.'s Spanish heritage and the emphatic connection of the house to its restful garden.

ABOVE: Lombardi combines classic furniture designs with another piece of McCall's modern wrought-iron work to create a simple composition in the living room. **BELOW:** Large stepping-stones form a path from the garage through a private garden to the main house. The flowers and greenery in the garden inspired the rich colors used throughout the house.

LEFT: The open design of Lombardi's house means that the living room, entry hall, and dining room are all part of one unbroken space. In the dining area, bent-plywood and wrought-iron chairs by Angelo Donghia surround a nineteenth-century Scandinavian country pine table. On the wall behind it is a composition of pipes designed by Lombardi. **RIGHT:** The loft at the top of the stairs serves as a bedroom. The architect added intriguing angles to the room when he positioned louvered closets on the loft wall. The screen in the corner is more wrought-iron work by McCall. The artworks above the bed are by Billy Al Bengston.

ROTONDI HOUSE

FAR LEFT: Architect Michael Rotondi calls this workspace he created in his family home "my own personal chapel." In an extraordinary skylit tower, Rotondi experiments with structural support using a cantilevered steel box beam and a twelve-by-twelve-inch wood beam.

TOP LEFT: A steel column at the entrance to Rotondi's office bisects the room. On the far side is a 7000-pound steel retaining wall that is wedged into the earth and, as Rotondi puts it, "forms a wall literally in balance with nature." Although functional elements are repeated in the room, such as the curved vertical supports on the plaster-and-glass side wall, none are identical. ABOVE LEFT: At square one, Rotondi's house was, in his words, an "anonymous stucco box" of about 1000 square feet. After the architect revised the original structure, increasing the space by fifty percent, the result was this inventive mix of geometric shapes formed with steel, glass, and wood. The exterior walls are covered in rolled asphalt roofing and steel plates that are waxed to achieve a unique sheen.

As times change, contemporary homes quickly become dated, pegged to a place in history—unless they are never completed and thus constantly in transition. Such is the case with the Rotondi House in Silver Lake, designed by architect Michael Rotondi for his family.

For Rotondi, part of the process was "to imagine, to build, to look, and to imagine again." A founding partner of Morphosis, one of the city's avant-garde architectural firms, and currently principal of his eponymous firm, Rotondi explains that this unconventional convergence of wood, steel, concrete, and glass has evolved since 1987 more from improvisation than from blueprints. "The house was constructed with minimal drawings—it was worked on, conceived, and built in full scale, in real time, simultaneously," he says.

Like much of Los Angeles, Silver Lake is a neighborhood with an architecturally demanding natural landscape. The steep slope at the back of the house required a retaining wall. Rather than build a predictable concrete block, Rotondi connected the house to the earth with a huge steel plane that becomes an art form as elegant as it is functional. As he notes, "Every practical decision is always an aesthetic one; anything that appears to be decorative is doing work."

When I asked my father why he chose Los Angeles to move to when he came from Italy, he answered, "Because I wanted to live in *America*." I think a lot of people see Los Angeles that way, as the most American place in America, the terminus for those in flight from homelands that economic, political, or personal situations have rendered uninhabitable. But it is not as if there is a preexisting civic character waiting to welcome the newcomers. Men and women come to Los Angeles because they want to live without capitulating to ready-made traditions and authorities, even if they are benevolent ones.

But the tradition of individualism would never be recognized as such if there weren't diverse, radically disjunct racial, ethnic, national, and linguistic cultures visibly informing the performance of individual liberty. Unsympathetic commentators seem unable to get beyond disapproval of how stubbornly these "foreign" identities resist dilution, and maintain that this has led to Los Angeles's decline into an irrelevant concentration of mutually antagonistic subaltern populations. And it's true that the absence of a tradition, language, rite, or anything else for its populations to share explodes the notion of community. An exclusive interest in cultivating the individual leaves responsibility for the form of the whole to chance. If there is a civics or politics to Los Angeles, it is largely unprogrammed, and by nature incoherent.

Two strategies have developed for negotiating this situation. One, that of the unsympathetic commentators, is based on suspicion and intolerance. Deceptively positive-sounding proposals would arbitrarily displace the region's authentic richness and tragedy with a fiction of the past—or with some defunct vision of the future. But political upheavals of the last few years have demonstrated to even the most obtuse collectivists and cultural conservatives that the imposition of cultural or stylistic or any other form of uniformity is not only a waste of effort but politically untenable.

An alternative strategy is being improvised in situ, as suggested by the activities documented in this book. In the neighborhood where I grew up, my friends were from Mexico, Japan, the South, the plains—and all those dinners with the different families added up to an education in the appropriateness of joining things that don't belong together. And now, as Los Angeles's cultural contrasts become even more striking, the appetite for engagement and enjoyment demonstrated by the kids who grow up in the city makes other responses seem narrow and incapacitated. This is both hopeful and necessary; unlike my friends and I, who grew up to discover that our experience of cultural juxtaposition was unusual, today's kids enter a world in which communication technologies are making such a situation ubiquitous.

Within this context, the role of the artist—whether legitimized as such or not—clearly involves celebration of this disunity, with a possible goal of transforming suspicion into festivity. For clues on how to accomplish this, the artists who are charged with building the environment can benefit from a sympathetic study of the buildings of non-architects. Operating without being informed by precedents and history, non-architects' directness and pragmatism often result in a fantastic poetry. Architects' more self-conscious designs reflect something of this spirit.

To understand what these homes are about, it is necessary to read the images thoughtfully, so as not to neglect the significance they have for their occupants. Though their field of action is confined to the boundaries of their piece of property, the expenditures of time and thought and commitment made by these architects and designers suggests what resources of talent are awaiting new challenges.

—Michael Rotondi

AFTERWORD

PHOTO CREDITS

SPRING